URBS

A COLLECTION OF LATIN PASSAGES SELECTED FROM
HISTORY, POETRY, SPEECHES, INSCRIPTIONS, AND
LETTERS WITH VOCABULARY, NOTES, AND QUESTIONS

COMPILED AND EDITED BY PAUL WHALEN

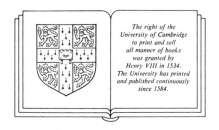

The right of the
University of Cambridge
to print and sell
all manner of books
was granted by
Henry VIII in 1534.
The University has printed
and published continuously
since 1584.

CAMBRIDGE UNIVERSITY PRESS

Cambridge

New York   Port Chester   Melbourne   Sydney

THEMES IN LATIN LITERATURE

amor et amicitia
imperium et civitas
multas per gentes
urbs antiqua

Published by the Press Syndicate of the University of Cambridge
The Pitt Building, Trumpington Street, Cambridge CB2 1RP
40 West 20th Street, New York, NY 10011, USA
10 Stamford Road, Oakleigh, Melbourne 3166, Australia

First published 1989 by Irwin Publishing Inc., Canada

This edition first published 1989

Printed in Great Britain at the University Press, Cambridge

British Library Cataloguing in Publication Data

Urbs antiqua: a collection of Latin
    passages selected from history, poetry,
    speeches, inscriptions and letters with
    vocabulary, notes and questions
    1. Latin – language – Readers
    I. Whalen, Paul
    478.6'421

Library of Congress Cataloging -in-Publication Data

Urbs antiqua: a collection of Latin passages selected from history,
    poetry, speeches, inscriptions, and letters, with vocabulary,
    notes, and questions/compiled and edited by Paul Whalen.
    English and Latin.
    Includes bibliographies.
    1. Latin language – Readers – City and town life.   2. Rome
    (Italy) – History – To 476 – Sources.   3. City and town life –
    History – Sources.   4. Cities and towns, Ancient – Sources.
    5. Latin literature.
    I. Whalen, Paul.
    PA2095.U7   1989
    478.6'421 – dc19

ISBN 0 521 37739 0

Cover Photograph: The cover shows a reconstruction of Imperial Rome with the Colosseum in the foreground and in the background the Capitoline Hill and the imperial fora. From a model of the city by I. Gismondi. (Rome, Museum of Roman Civilization)

Maps and illustrations by Tibor Kovalik

Text and cover design by Brant Cowie/Artplus Ltd.
Typeset by Jay Tee Graphics Ltd.

Table of Contents

DEDICATION

For my wife, Anna, and my children

ACKNOWLEDGEMENTS

The author would like to thank the following people whose advice and comments were particularly helpful in the preparation of *urbs antiqua*.

Donald E. Sprague
Loyola Academy
Wilmette, Illinois

Professor John E. Stambaugh
Williams College
Williamstown, Massachusetts

Professor Alexander Dalzell
Trinity College
University of Toronto
Toronto, Ontario

Professor Alexander G. McKay
McMaster University
Hamilton, Ontario

NOTE TO THE TEACHER

This text is designed to provide you with readings suitable for students beginning to read original Latin. The Latin of all the selections is either unadapted or only very mildly edited. What editing there is usually takes the form of deletion rather than alteration.

Over 400 lines are offered here for an investigation of the theme of *urbs antiqua*. Additional passages for further exploration of each aspect of the theme are given at the end of each subtopic. A number of Pliny's Letters from Bithynia that describe various civic forms may be found in *imperium et civitas*, a text prepared by Patricia E. Bell for this same series, *Themes in Latin Literature*.

Each selection is an independent unit with its own vocabulary and notes. Therefore it is not necessary to read every selection or to handle the selections in the order presented here. I have attempted to include a variety of genres and authors and of passages known and not so well known, long and short, serious and humorous, easy and difficult.

The Discussion Questions at the end of each subtopic are intended to be directional, not comprehensive, and can be modified to suit your selected prose and poetry readings. The questions are designed to explore the surface meaning of a passage, to compare the effectiveness of one literary piece with another in a subtopic, and to develop a deeper understanding of the subtopic and its relationship to the general theme of the ancient city.

Finally, the link between archaeological remains and literary remains as means of understanding the theme of the ancient city is paramount. Consequently, access to visual resources is essential as well as the use of Vitruvius' *De Architectura* as a central reference text for providing the rationale, building principles and practices, characteristics, and functions of Roman civic structures.

TO THE STUDENT

*U*rbs antiqua is designed to explore the natural political and social unit of the Roman—the city. By combining archaeological and literary evidence, you will come to understand what Romans saw and felt about the urban environment. The book focuses on life in the city, urban planning and expansion, and the major Roman civic forms such as the forum, basilica, temple, amphitheatre, and baths. The Romans can be seen working as barber, lawyer, gladiator, or charioteer, walking to their patrons' houses for the "*salutatio*" or "*sportula*," listening to hawkers sell their wares in street shops, watching gladiators fight at the games, and taking a bath. The people's attitudes towards city life are included in the selection of passages, which take the form of elegy, epigram, epistle, history, inscription, satire, and technical treatise.

For purposes of discussion and comparison, the selected passages are divided into four subtopics of the theme of the ancient city: The City — Ideology and Planning; Urban Structures — Forum, Basilica, Temple, Market, and Baths; Life in the City; and Spectacula.

Notes and vocabulary have been included to assist you in translating each passage. To appreciate the relationship of sound to sense, an oral reading, both in prose and in poetry, is essential not only at your initial exploration but also at the end with your discussion and analysis.

The Initial Questions at the end of each subtopic are intended to consolidate comprehension after you have worked through a passage. An analysis of the writer's treatment of the theme is expected in your class discussion. Many questions require you to quote from the Latin text words and phrases that support your viewpoint.

The Discussion Questions are designed to compare and contrast the different writers' concepts of the theme and their effectiveness and distinctiveness as writers; to help you understand the subtopic and its relationship to the theme; to encourage you to study archaeological evidence and thereby develop a sense of the relationship between the literary and the archaeological record of urban life; and, finally, to help you to form analogies between the ancient Roman city and cities today. Many questions do not have a clear-cut "correct" answer, and are intended to provoke discussion. In this way, you will learn not only to appreciate a literary work in its own right, but also to reflect on what it tells the reader about one's own experience of living in a town or city.

GLOSSARY OF SOME LITERARY TERMS USED IN *THEMES IN LATIN LITERATURE*

In writing a literary appreciation for a piece of literature, it is not enough simply to list literary devices and examples. Always examine critically each device to see *how* the writer uses it and *what* effect is achieved by its use in that context.

anaphora: the repetition of an important word at the beginning of several successive clauses

alliteration: the repetition of the same sound, usually a consonant, at the beginning of two or more adjacent words

antithesis: a rhetorical contrast achieved by the balanced or parallel arrangement of words, clauses, or sentences with a strong contrast in meaning

assonance: the repetition of the same vowel sounds in two or more adjacent words

asyndeton: the omission of conjunctions or customary connecting words

atmosphere: the mood pervading the literary work

cadence: a measured rhythmic sequence or flow of words in prose or poetry

connotation: the cluster of implicit or associated meanings of a word as distinguished from that word's denotative or specific meaning

diction: the deliberate choice of words

ellipsis: the omission of word(s) necessary for the grammatical structure of a sentence

emphatic word order:

   (i)   **chiasmus**: a criss-cross arrangement usually resulting from the separation of two nouns and the adjectives that modify each

   (ii)   **first and last word positions**: placing an important word at these emphatic positions in a line of poetry

   (iii)   **framing**: a word placed out of its usual order and "framed" by a pair of related words to make the word stand out prominently

   (iv)   **interlocking word order**: the words of one noun-adjective phrase alternating with those of another

   (v)   **juxtaposition**: two words or phrases set side by side to intensify meaning

   (vi)   **separation**: separating grammatically related words (e.g., noun—noun, noun—adjective) to produce a word picture of the meaning conveyed by the words

epic: a long narrative poem in elevated style, typically having as its subject a hero on whose exploits depends to some degree the fate of a nation or race

epic simile: a comparison extended beyond the obvious comparison by further details

epigram: a brief and pointed poem, usually ending with a surprising or witty turn of thought

figurative language: language that departs from the literal standard meaning in order to achieve a special effect, e.g., metaphor, personification, simile

genre: a literary form, e.g., epic, lyric, satire

hyperbole: an extravagant exaggeration of fact used to express strong feeling and not intended to be taken literally

imagery: the poetic technique of making mental pictures in such a way as to make the emotion or mood appeal vividly to the reader and to produce a clue to poetic intent

interjection: a sudden phrase or word that interrupts the grammatical progress of the sentence

irony: the use of words that convey a sense or attitude contrary to what is literally expressed; e.g., often ostensible praise or approval implies condemnation or contempt

metaphor: an indirect comparison whereby one thing is compared to another without the expressed indication of the point of similarity

mythological allusion: a brief reference to mythological details the writer assumes will be readily recognized by the reader instead of stating directly the myth or name of the person or thing

onomatopoeia or imitative harmony: the use of a word whose sound resembles the sound it describes

oxymoron: a rhetorical contrast achieved by putting together two contradictory terms

paradox: a statement that seems contradictory but that reveals a coherent truth

parallelism or balanced structure: the recurrence or repetition of a grammatical pattern

pathos: the creation of pity or sorrow in the reader

periodic sentence: a sentence designed to arouse interest and suspense by keeping the meaning unclear until the very end

personification: the description of an inanimate object or concept in terms of human qualities

rhetoric: the presentation of ideas in a persuasive manner, usually used for effectiveness in oratory or public speaking; for specific rhetoric devices, see anaphora, alliteration, etc.

rhetorical question: a question used for its persuasive effect and for which no answer is expected or for which the answer is self-evident; it is used to achieve rhetorical emphasis stronger than a direct statement

rhythm: the pattern of long and short syllables in each line of poetry

rhyme: the repetition of the same sound at the end of two or more words

satire: a literary form in which prevailing vices or follies are held up to humour and ridicule and evoke towards them attitudes of amusement, indignation, or contempt

simile: a stated comparison often indicated by a term such as *velut*, *similis*, or *qualis*. A simile extended to embellish, complete, or reinforce the narrative with a vivid picture, the details of which are not always relevant to the original point of comparison, is called an **epic simile**.

theme: the central or dominating idea of a literary work

tone: the attitude of the writer to the subject. The tone may be characterized, for example, as formal or informal, solemn or playful, satirical, serious, or ironic.

transferred epithet: the application of a significant modifier to a word other than the one to which it actually belongs

vivid particularization: a concrete or specified description, usually achieved by the use of proper nouns rich in connotations

SHORT BIOGRAPHIES OF LATIN AUTHORS QUOTED IN *URBS ANTIQUA*

Cicero: Orator, Statesman, Philosopher, Letter Writer (106 B.C.-43 B.C.)

Marcus Tullius Cicero was born in Arpinum, southeast of Rome, of a family of equestrian rank. He studied rhetoric and philosophy in Rome, the culminating subjects of Roman education. Beginning with his successful prosecution of the Roman governor Verres in 70 B.C., Cicero used his success as a lawyer to advance politically through the various grades of public office to the consulship in 63 B.C. and governorship of Cilicia in 52 B.C. He was proscribed and killed by the Second Triumvirate in 43 B.C.

As well as being the greatest of Roman orators, Cicero was a prolific writer who left us forensic and political speeches, theoretical works on rhetoric and philosophy, and nearly 800 letters. Cicero is known for his periodic style with a sentence structure often consisting of an orderly development of thought, a string of balanced subordinate clauses and rhetorical figures of speech. It is because of his voluminous literary works, especially his letters and speeches, that we know more about his life and his age than about any other period of Roman history.

Juvenal: Satirist (c. A.D. 55-c. A.D. 128)

Decimus Iunius Iuvenalis, son of a wealthy freedman, came from Aquinum, a town about 130 km southeast of Rome. Biographical details provided by ancient sources are contradictory. Like his friend and fellow poet, Martial, Juvenal spent some time in Rome as a poor client dependent on the doles of the wealthy. He was probably exiled by Domitian to Egypt for lampooning a court favourite, the dancer Paris. Later Juvenal returned to Rome where he probably acquired a modest income and property from his writings and generous patrons.

In writing his five books of *Satires*, Juvenal described Rome as he knew it. Using an invective tone, the poet writes as a social observer in the form of protest and not as a remedy. His style is marked by a line of argument followed by examples, graphic realism, poetic imagination, cutting phrases, and memorable epigrams such as "a healthy mind in a healthy body." Juvenal was to become a model for satirists during and after the Renaissance.

Livy: Historian (59 B.C.-A.D. 17)

Titus Livius, born at Patavium (Padua) in northern Italy, came to Rome in about 31 B.C., and spent most of his life there. Little is known about his family background except that he had a son and daughter. We do know that he devoted his long life to writing a monumental history of Rome from its foundation to 9 B.C.

Public readings of his work apparently brought him fame and, ultimately, contact with Augustus who, in establishing a new order based on republican traditions, expressed an interest in the historian's forty-year task. A tombstone inscription found at Padua confirms Livy's retirement to his native city and death there.

Most of Livy's work, known as *Ab Urbe Condita*, has been lost, but the 35 out of 142 books that survive provide the reader with the story of Rome's rise to power in Italy and of the long struggle against the Carthaginian, Hannibal. By describing the morals and the deeds of individuals and of the nation, he wanted to instill in his fellow Romans a pride in their glorious past and likewise a belief in a glorious future under the reign of Augustus. Livy's lively writing style included many poetic words, varied sentence structure, vivid details, moral episodes, and rhetorical speeches. As an historical critic, Livy is condemned for his careless use of annalistic sources and his inaccurate description of battles and of geography. As an historical writer, his literary merits are evident in the portrayal of events, moods, and characters in an instructive, patriotic manner.

Martial: Epigrammatist (c. A.D. 40-c. A.D. 104)

Marcus Valerius Martialis, born and educated in Spain, left the dull life of his provincial hill town of Bilbilis and went to Rome in A.D. 64 to enjoy the attractions of a large, cosmopolitan city and to seek a wider scope for his writing abilities. During his thirty-five-year stay in Rome, he led the ordinary life of a needy client using his wit, charm and poetry to curry the favour of various patrons. He never ceased to complain about the client's duties such as calling on his patron in the morning and accompanying him on his social and business round. At first poor, Martial lived in a third-floor lodging, but later, when his poetry earned him an income from booksellers and generous patrons, he acquired a small house on the Quirinal Hill, and at Nomentum, northeast of Rome, a farm tiny enough, as he says, to hide under the wing of a cricket. About A.D. 100, tired of city living, Martial, with Pliny the Younger's financial help, returned to Bilbilis to a quiet country life on a farm given to him by a wealthy patroness. He died there soon afterwards.

His poems, of which more than 1500 survive, provide realistic glimpses of everyday life. His writings include: (1) *Liber Spectaculorum*, published in A.D. 80, describing the combats in the arena commemorating the opening of the Flavian amphitheatre (Colosseum) by Titus; (2) mottoes to accompany gifts sent to friends (*Xenia*) or taken home from banquets (*Apophoreta*) on the festival of the Saturnalia; (3) *Epigrammaton libri*, 12 books of epigrams providing realistic glimpses of everyday life. Martial understood and described human behaviour in an amusing and tolerant fashion. His writing style employed wit, charm, terse phrases, exaggeration, and antithesis. He is known as the father of the epigram in its modern sense for ending many of his short poems with an unexpected twist or witty point.

Ovid: Poet (43 B.C.-A.D. 17)

Publius Ovidius Naso, born of an equestrian family at Sulmo, 145 km east of Rome, studied rhetoric and law at Rome and philosophy at Athens. After holding minor official posts, he abandoned public life in favour of writing poetry and soon was recognized as the leading poet in Rome. In A.D. 8, Ovid fell into disfavour with Augustus and was banished to Tomis on the Black Sea where he passed the remainder of his life.

Ovid's works fall into three groups. His love poetry, including the *Amores*, are elegies which, like our selection, light-heartedly describe Ovid's courtship of a girl. His poems of Greek mythology and Roman legends include the *Fasti*, which is a poetic interpretation of the Roman civil, religious, and astronomical calendar from January to June with its accompanying rituals, festivals, and traditions. The poems of his exile include the *Epistulae ex Ponto*, which are full of nostalgia for his life in Rome, complaints about his dreary exile, and pleas to Augustus for pardon. It was Ovid's power to capture human emotion and to isolate the important moment in a dramatic scene or episode that influenced later artists and writers and entertained readers of all ages.

Pliny the Younger: Letter Writer and Statesman (c. A.D. 61-c. A.D. 112)

Gaius Plinius Caecilius Secundus, son of a wealthy landowner of Comum (Como) in northern Italy, was later adopted and brought up by his uncle, Pliny the Elder. Pliny was a studious youth who at 14 wrote a Greek tragedy and at about 18 preferred to quietly study during Vesuvius' great eruption rather than accompany his uncle on his fatal inspection. He studied rhetoric at Rome under the famous teacher, Quintilian. As a successful lawyer, Pliny frequently pleaded for his clients' inheritances in the Centumviral Court and acted as state prosecutor against provincial governors charged with extortion. His senatorial career culminated in a consulship in A.D. 100, and the governorship of Bithynia (now part of Turkey) in A.D. 110. He was to reorganize the badly managed province, where he apparently died in office.

During his career in public life, Pliny published his speeches and letters. Pliny's contribution to Roman literature is the over 200 surviving letters which describe the private and public life of a kind, generous, noble gentleman who counted among his friends Tacitus and Suetonius. His correspondence with Trajan provides a valuable insight into the administration of an imperial province. The style of his letters is characterized by logic, simplicity, brevity and frankness.

Seneca: Philosopher and Politician (c. 4 B.C.-A.D. 65)

Lucius Annaeus Seneca, son of a wealthy equestrian, was born at Corduba in southern Spain. Receiving a formal education in Rome, Seneca embarked on a career which led him to become a wealthy money-lender, imperial tutor and chief minister of Nero, and Stoic philosopher. While in retirement, Seneca was forced to commit suicide for alleged complicity in a plot to overthrow Nero in A.D. 65.

A man of wide learning and interests, Seneca wrote on various subjects and in various genres: science, philosophy, tragedy, satire, essay, letter and epigram. His most popular prose work, the 124 *Epistulae Morales* to his friend Lucilius, consists of brief moral philosophical essays on various aspects of contemporary Roman life such as riches, happiness, death and suicide, travel, baths, and the games. Advocating Stoic principles, these didactic essays attempt to answer the primary philosophical question of how people ought to conduct their lives. Seneca's informal writing style exhibits balance, pointed wit, epigrammatic brevity, colloquialisms, and anecdotes.

Suetonius: Biographer (c. A.D. 69-c. A.D. 140)

Gaius Suetonius Tranquillus, whose family probably came from Hippo Regius in Numidia (Annaba in Algeria), may have at various times in his career taught literature, practised law, and served on the staff of Pliny the Younger, governor of Bithynia. Subsequently he joined the imperial service and held the posts of director of the imperial libraries under Trajan and private secretary under Hadrian. But in A.D. 121/2 he was dismissed for some breach of court etiquette. Thereafter, he devoted himself to his literary career.

Suetonius was a scholarly, prolific writer, but the majority of his works on grammar, rhetoric, archaeology, natural history, and physical science have perished. His extant *De Vita Caesarum*, twelve biographies from Julius Caesar to Domitian, was published under Hadrian in A.D. 120. Unlike the ancient historians who concentrated on war, politics, and great events, Suetonius concerned himself with the life, personality, and achievement of each emperor, illustrated by lively anecdotes. A studious and careful compiler of facts from relevant documents including imperial files, Suetonius writes his biography in an objective manner with an absence of the moralistic judgements associated with the historians Livy and Tacitus. He uses simple language and grammatical constructions to provide a rapid, dramatic, anecdotal narrative. His clear style and the intrinsic interest in his subject have made him one of the most widely read of classical authors.

Tacitus: Historian and Statesman (c. A.D. 56-c. A.D. 117)

Publius Cornelius Tacitus, born in Gaul or northern Italy, studied rhetoric in Rome and soon became one of the best-known speakers of his time in the law courts and in the senate. At the age of twenty-two, he married the daughter of Agricola, then consul and soon to be governor of Britain. Armed with this family link, he soon held the high positions of state prosecutor, praetor, consul and provincial governor.

Tacitus' literary works include the *Annals*, which narrate the rule of the Julio-Claudian emperors from Tiberius to Nero (A.D. 14-68); the *Histories*, which describe the rule of the emperors from Galba to Domitian (A.D. 69-96); and the *Agricola* (A.D. 98), a biography about his father-in-law's exploits in Britain. The sources for his works are the writers of annals, formal histories, memoirs, state papers, senatorial archives and speeches, and personal reminiscences. Tacitus' historical writings display a moral purpose and keen insight into character and events. His gifts of pictorial description and psychological analysis are illustrated by his portrayal of Nero and the great fire of Rome. His mastery of atmosphere, noble style, command of evidence, and sense of history and accuracy made Tacitus the premier Roman historian.

Tertullian: Christian Writer (c. A.D. 160-c. A.D. 240)

Quintus Septimius Florens Tertullianus of Carthage was the first Christian theologian to write extensively in Latin. Influenced by the courage of Christian martyrs, Tertullian was converted to Christianity about A.D. 195 and thereafter devoted himself to writing in defence of Christianity against pagan and heretical attacks and about the Christian way of life. In his early work, *De Spectaculis*, Tertullian distinguishes the Christian from the pagan way of life by explaining why his fellow Christians should not attend theatrical productions, races, and gladiatorial games. While devoting himself to moral and ethical problems, Tertullian wrote against the charges of atheism and black magic levied against Christians. The 31 surviving works of this prolific writer have had a profound impact on religious and political thought in the West.

Vitruvius: Architect and Military Engineer (First Century B.C.)

Vitruvius Pollio, who served in the army with Julius Caesar and later under Augustus, wrote the architectural and engineering treatise *De Architectura*. Although written during Augustus' reign, Vitruvius' textbook is marked by no reference to any buildings of Augustan Rome. Divided into ten books, his work includes topics like the architect's qualifications and training, town planning, building materials and methods, form and function of public and domestic buildings, interior decoration, hydraulic engineering, time-measuring devices, and machinery for war and industry. Vitruvius' handbook of architecture provides the reader with a basis to analyze building tasks and finished products. It is the only technical monograph on architecture to have survived from the Roman world.

PART I
THE CITY—IDEOLOGY AND PLANNING

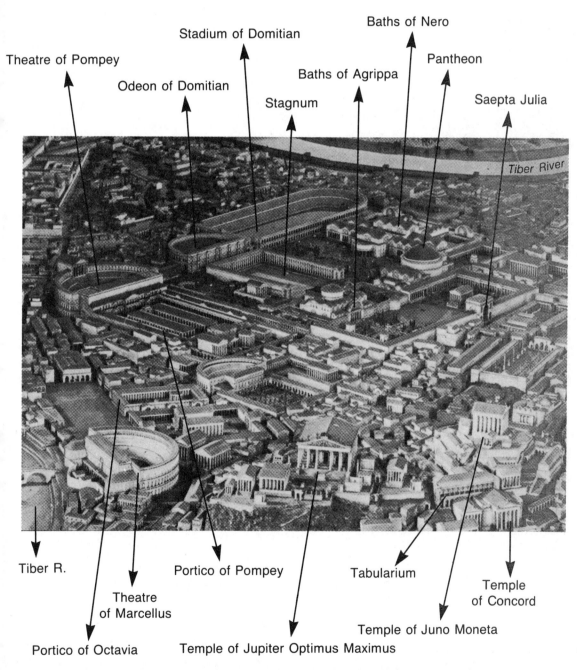

Baths of Nero

Stadium of Domitian

Theatre of Pompey

Pantheon

Odeon of Domitian

Baths of Agrippa

Stagnum

Saepta Julia

Tiber River

Tiber R.

Portico of Pompey

Tabularium

Temple
of Concord

Theatre
of Marcellus

Temple of Juno Moneta

Portico of Octavia

Temple of Jupiter Optimus Maximus

This photograph shows a reconstruction of Imperial Rome in the Campus Martius area. From a model of the city by I. Gismondi. (Rome, Museum of Roman Civilization)

AUGUSTUS

cum adtenderem te non solum de vita communi
omnium curam publicaeque rei constitutionem habere
sed etiam de opportunitate publicorum aedificiorum,
ut civitas per te non solum provinciis esset aucta,
verum etiam ut maiestas imperii publicorum aedificio- 5
rum egregias haberet auctoritates, non putavi praetermittendum, quin primo quoque tempore de his rebus
ea tibi ederem.

Vitruvius, *De Architectura* Preface

THE PARTS OF ARCHITECTURE

partes ipsius architecturae sunt tres: aedificatio,
gnomonice, machinatio. aedificatio autem divisa est
bipertito, e quibus una est moenium et communium
operum in publicis locis conlocatio, altera est privato-
rum aedificiorum explicatio. publicorum autem dis- 5
tributiones sunt tres, e quibus est una defensionis,
altera religionis, tertia opportunitatis. defensionis est
murorum turriumque et portarum ratio ad hostium
impetus perpetuo repellendos excogitata, religionis
deorum immortalium fanorum aediumque sacrarum 10
conlocatio, opportunitatis communium locorum ad
usum publicum dispositio, uti portus, fora, porticus,
balinea, theatra, inambulationes ceteraque, quae isdem
rationibus in publicis locis designantur.

(continued on page 4)

Augustus

In the Preface to his *De Architectura*, Vitruvius points out how important Augustus thought his building program in the city of Rome was to establishing his own image as emperor and the city's image as the centre of an empire. In order to reflect the greatness and generosity of the emperor, Rome must look like an imperial capital and set a standard of urban beauty to match its political importance. The ideology and the building activities of Rome's first emperor were a source of inspiration for later emperors, who tried to emulate them not only in Rome itself but also throughout the vast empire.

---

adtendo, ere consider
communis, e common
res publica, rei publicae, f state
constitutio, onis, f constitution
opportunitas, atis, f lit., opportunity (here "provision"): Augustus rightly boasted that he found a Rome built of brick and left one clothed in marble (Suetonius, *Augustus* 29)
augeo, ere, auxi, auctus become greater

5 *maiestas, atis, f* majesty, greatness
egregius, a, um eminent, distinguished
habeo, ere express, produce
auctoritas, atis, f authority, dignity
non putavi praetermittendum Tr. "I thought the opportunity should not be missed"
ea Tr. "my writings," "my proposals" (*i.e.*, his handbook on architecture)
edo, ere present

The Parts of Architecture

In describing the parts of architecture, Vitruvius outlines the types of building to be built and the importance of using strength, utility, and grace in their construction. The architect arranged the buildings outlined here by paying attention to mass and space, the basic elements of architectural design. The success of the architectural work of a city like Rome is determined by how skilfully its designers combine architectural forms, materials, colour, modulation of light and shade, and texture both in the interior spaces and in the spaces around the buildings.

---

aedificatio, onis, f building
gnomonice, es, f science of sundials
machinatio, onis, f mechanics
bipertito, adv. in two parts
moenia, ium, n. pl. city walls
communis, e public
locum, i, n site
conlocatio, onis, f placing, siting
5 *explicatio, onis, f* laying out, planning
distributio, onis, f assignment, distribution
opportunitas, atis, f convenience
turris, is, f tower
ratio, onis, f there are 3 meanings in this passage: (a) system (line 8), "a system of walls, etc."; (b) purpose, principle (line 14), "for the same purposes"; (c) *ratio-*

nem habere + gen (lines 15 and 16), "to take account of"
perpetuo, adv. constantly, continuously
excogito, are, avi, atus devise, think out
10 *fanum, i, n* shrine
aedes, is, f temple
dispositio, onis, f spatial arrangement, layout: according to Vitruvius, "*dispositio*" involves the harmonization of ground-plan, elevation, and perspective
porticus, us, f colonnade
balineum i, n bath
inambulatio, onis, f promenade
designo, are mark out, plan

3

haec autem ita fieri debent, ut habeatur ratio firmi- 15
tatis, utilitatis, venustatis. firmitatis erit habita ratio,
cum fuerit fundamentorum ad solidum depressio, qua-
que e materia, copiarum sine avaritia diligens electio;
utilitatis autem, cum fuerit emendata et sine impedi-
tione usus locorum dispositio et ad regiones sui cui- 20
usque generis apta et commoda distributio; venustatis
vero, cum fuerit operis species grata et elegans mem-
brorumque commensus iustas habeat symmetriarum
ratiocinationes.

Vitruvius, *De Architectura* I.iii

THE SITE OF ROME

"non sine causa di hominesque hunc urbi condendae
locum elegerunt, saluberrimos colles, flumen oppor-
tunum, quo ex mediterraneis locis fruges devehantur,
quo maritimi commeatus accipiantur, mari vicinum
ad commoditates nec expositum nimia propinquitate 5
ad pericula classium externarum, regionem Italiae
mediam, ad incrementum urbis natum unice locum."
   antiquata deinde lege, promisce urbs aedificari
coepta. tegula publice praebita est; saxi materiaeque
caedendae, unde quisque vellet ius factum, praedibus 10
acceptis eo anno aedificia perfecturos. festinatio curam
exemit vicos dirigendi, dum omisso sui alienique dis-
crimine in vacuo aedificant. ea est causa ut veteres
cloacae, primo per publicum ductae, nunc privata passim subeant tecta, formaque urbis sit occupatae magis 15
quam divisae similis.

Livy, *Ab Urbe Condita* V.54-55

15 *fio, fieri* be done, be accomplished
firmitas, atis, f strength
utilitas, atis, f usefulness
venustas, atis, f charm, grace
fundamentum, i, n foundation
ad solidum Tr. "to the solid ground"
depressio, onis, f a digging down
quisque, quaeque, quodque each
copiae, arum, f. pl. supplies
sine avaritia Tr. "without penny-
  pinching"
electio, onis, f choice
20 *utilitatis...distributio* Tr. "(Account will be

taken) of utility, when there is a correct arrangement of places without any
hindrance to use, and when there is a
fit and suitable arrangement in relation
to the geographic location (*regio*) of
each type"
species, ei, f appearance
membrum, i, n part
commensus, us, m relative measurements,
  scale
iustus, a, um proper, right
symmetriae, arum, f. pl. symmetry
ratiocinatio, onis, f calculation

The Site of Rome

After the Gauls sacked Rome in the early fourth century B.C., a proposal to move its site was successfully resisted by the Roman leader Camillus, who spoke to the people from the Rostra. A portion of Camillus' speech and an account of the early stages of the rebuilding of Rome can be found in this passage.

condo, ere found
saluberrimus, a, um very healthy
opportunus, a, um convenient
mediterraneus, a, um inland
fruges, frugum, f crops, produce
deveho, ere carry down
commeatus, us, m. pl. supplies, provisions
vicinus, a, um neighbouring
5 *commoditas, atis, f* convenience,
  advantage
nimius, a, um too much
propinquitas, atis, f nearness
externus, a, um foreign
incrementum, i, n growth, expansion
natum unice Tr. "uniquely adapted"
antiquo, are, avi, atus reject
lex, legis, f bill
promisce indiscriminately, in random
  fashion
tegula, ae, f tiles

publice at the state's expense
praebeo, ere, ui, itus supply
materia, ae, f timber
10 *caedo, ere* hew, carve
ius, iuris, n right
factum (est) was granted
praes, praedis, m security, pledge
praedibus acceptis (eos)...perfecturos (esse)
festinatio, onis, f haste
eximo, ere, exemi remove
vicus, i, m street
dirigo, ere lay straight
dum until
alienum, i, n property of another
discrimen, inis, n distinction
vacuum, i, n unassigned land
cloaca, ae, f sewer
15 *passim, adv.* in every direction
tectum, i, n dwelling, house
forma, ae, f appearance

The Fire of Rome

I THE FIRE ITSELF

sequitur clades, utrum forte an dolo principis incertum (nam utrumque auctores prodidere), sed omnibus quae huic urbi per violentiam ignium acciderunt gravior atque atrocior. initium in ea parte circi ortum quae Palatino Caelioque montibus contigua est, ubi 5 per tabernas, quibus id mercimonium inerat quo flamma alitur. ignis statim validus ac vento citus longitudinem circi corripuit. neque enim domus munimentis saeptae vel templa muris cincta aut quid aliud morae interiacebat. impetu pervagatum incen- 10 dium plana primum, deinde in edita adsurgens et rursus inferiora populando, anteiit remedia velocitate mali et obnoxia urbe artis itineribus hucque et illuc flexis atque enormibus vicis, qualis vetus Roma fuit.

  ad hoc erant lamenta paventium feminarum, qui- 15 que sibi aut aliis consulebant, dum trahunt invalidos aut opperiuntur, pars mora, pars festinans, cuncta impediebant. et saepe dum in tergum respectant lateribus aut fronte circumveniebantur. postremo, quid vitarent quid peterent ambigui, complere vias, sterni 20 per agros. alii amissis omnibus fortunis, alii caritate suorum, quos eripere nequiverant, quamvis patente effugio interiere. nec quisquam defendere audebat, crebris multorum minis restinguere prohibentium, et quia alii palam faces iaciebant atque esse sibi auctorem 25 vociferabantur, sive ut raptus licentius exercerent seu iussu.

Tacitus, Annals XV.38

The Fire of Rome

The great fire of Rome in A.D. 64, the most spectacular event in the reign of Nero (A.D. 54-68), is of interest to us in three ways: (1) it illustrates the ever-present danger of extensive damage by fire to an ancient city; (2) it provided Nero with the opportunity to draw up an urban-renewal project that was to shape the city until the end of the empire; (3) it became an excuse for Nero's brutal persecution of Christians, whom Nero blamed for starting the fire.

I The Fire Itself

On the night of a full moon on July 18, the fire broke out while Nero was at his favourite country retreat at Antium near Naples.

---

clades, is, f disaster, calamity
forte by chance, accidentally
dolus, i, m wrongdoing
princeps, ipis, m emperor
auctor, oris, m reporter, author
prodo, ere, prodidi hand down, record
ortum = ortum (est) arose
5 *contiguus, a, um* neighbouring, adjoining
mercimonium, ii, n merchandise
insum, inesse be contained in
quo flamma alitur Tr. "inflammable":
  modifying "*mercimonium*"
validus, a, um strong, powerful
citus, a, um stirred, fanned
corripio, ere, ripui sweep
munimentum, i, n boundary wall
saeptus, a, um fenced in, enclosed
vel or
cingo, ere, xi, cinctus surround
10 *quid aliud morae* Tr. "any other obstacle"
interiaceo, ere lie between
incendium, ii, n conflagration
impetus, us, m sweep, wide extent of space
pervagatum = pervagatum (est) spread
  through
planum, i, n flat or level ground
editum, i, n height
adsurgo, ere rise
populo, are devastate
anteeo, anteire, anteii go before, outstrip
obnoxia...itineribus Tr. "the city being
  vulnerable by reason of narrow paths"
flexus, a, um winding

enormis, e irregular
vicus, i, m street: often less than 4.80 m
  wide; tenement buildings, lining the
  narrow streets, created an air draught
  to sweep the fire along and provided
  fuel for its increase
15 *ad hoc* besides
lamentum, i, n wailing, weeping
pavens, entis terrified
consulo, ere + dat. take care of, look to
opperior, iri wait
cuncta everything
20 *complere and sterni* hist. infs.
sterno, ere fling down, throw to the
  ground
caritas, atis, f love
sui, orum, m family, loved ones
nequeo, ire, ivi be unable
patens, entis open, accessible
effugium, ii, n a means of escape
interiere = interierunt perished
defendere Tr. "to check the fire"
creber, bra, brum frequent
minis, abl. of cause by threats
restinguo, ere extinguish, put out
25 *palam, adv.* openly
esse sibi auctorem Tr. "that they acted
  under orders"
vociferor, ari cry out, shout out
sive...seu whether...or
raptus, us, m plundering, looting
licentius, adv. more freely, more boldly
exerceo, ere practise, engage in

II THE AFTERMATH

eo in tempore Nero Antii agens non ante in urbem
regressus est quam domui eius, qua Palatium et Maecenatis hortos continuaverat, ignis propinquaret. neque
tamen sisti potuit quin et Palatium et domus et cuncta
circum haurirentur. sed solacium populo exturbato ac 5
profugo campum Martis ac monumenta Agrippae,
hortos quin etiam suos patefecit et subitaria aedificia
exstruxit quae multitudinem inopem acciperent; sub-
vectaque utensilia ab Ostia et propinquis municipiis
pretiumque frumenti minutum usque ad ternos 10
nummos. quae quamquam popularia in inritum cade-
bant, quia pervaserat rumor ipso tempore flagrantis
urbis iniisse eum domesticam scaenam et cecinisse
Troianum excidium, praesentia mala vetustis cladibus
adsimulantem.   15

  sexto demum die apud imas Esquilias finis incendio
factus, prorutis per immensum aedificiis, ut continuae
violentiae campus et velut vacuum caelum occurreret.
necdum positus metus aut redierat plebi spes: rursum
grassatus ignis patulis magis urbis locis; eoque strages 20
hominum erat minor, delubra deorum et porticus
amoenitati dicatae latius procidere. plusque infamiae
id incendium habuit quia praediis Tigellini Aemilianis
proruperat videbaturque Nero condendae urbis novae
et cognomento suo appellandae gloriam quaerere. 25
quippe in regiones quattuordecim Roma dividitur,
quarum quattuor integrae manebant, tres solo tenus
deiectae: septem reliquis pauca tectorum vestigia
supererant, lacera et semusta.

                                  Tacitus, *Annals* XV.39-40

II The Aftermath

Although the Capitol and the Forum escaped damage, there were extensive losses in lives, in residential buildings, in venerable monuments from early Rome such as the Temple of Vesta, and in many Greek art treasures.

ago, ere be (passive: of units of time)

continuo, are, avi connect together

propinquo, are approach

Maecenatis hortos the gardens of Maecenas on the Esquiline Hill were part of the imperial grounds

quin + subj. Tr. "from"

sisto, ere stop

5 *haurio, ire* consume, devour

solacium, ii, n comfort

exturbatus, a, um driven out

profugus, a, um fleeing

monumenta Agrippae the public buildings of Agrippa included in the Campus Martius a fancy shopping area (*Saepta*), a *thermae*, the Basilica Neptune, and the Pantheon

quin etiam nay even, indeed

patefacio, ere, feci throw open

subitarius, a, um temporary, emergency

inops, inopis helpless, destitute

subvectus, a, um carried upstream

utensilia, orum, n. pl. necessities

propinquus, a, um neighbouring

municipium, ii, n town

0 *minutus, a, um* reduced

ternus, a, um three

nummus, i, m sesterce: a coin of small value

quae Tr. "these relief measures"

in inritum of no effect

cado, ere turn out

pervado, ere, si pervade, spread

ineo, ire, ii enter, appear

domesticus, a, um private

scaena, ae, f stage: it is this account that is at the root of the popular image of Nero fiddling while Rome burns; Tacitus reports the account as a rumour while Suetonius (*Nero* 38) affirms it as a fact

cano, ere, cecini sing (*i.e.*, perform)

excidium, ii, n destruction

vetus, eris ancient

15 *adsimulo, are* compare

proruo, ere, rui, rutus demolish

per immensum over a vast area

campus et velut vacuum caelum a Tacitean hyperbole: Tr. "a flat field and as it were an open sky"

necdum positus (erat)

20 *grassor, ari, atus sum* rage

patulus, a, um open

strages, is, f toll, loss

delubrum, i, n shrine, temple

amoenitas, atis, f pleasure

dicatus, a, um devoted, dedicated

procido, ere, idi fall down

praedium, ii, n estate

Tigellinus, i, m Tigellinus was the hated head of the Praetorian Guard

Aemilianus, a, um Aemiliana is a district on the northwest side of the Capitoline Hill

prorumpo, ere, prorupi break out

videor, eri seem

condo, ere found

25 *cognomentum, i, n* surname, *cognomen*

quippe indeed

integer, gra, grum intact, uninjured

solum, i, n ground

tenus + abl. right up to, as far as

deiectae (sunt) were razed, were levelled

vestigia, orum, n. pl. ruins, traces

supersum, esse survive

lacer, era, erum shattered, wrecked, gutted

semustus, a, um half burned out

III THE REBUILDING OF ROME

PART 1: *DOMUS AUREA*

non in alia re tamen fuit damnosior quam in
aedificando. domum a Palatio Esquilias usque fecit,
quam primo transitoriam, mox incendio absumptam
restitutamque auream nominavit. de cuius spatio atque
cultu suffecerit haec rettulisse. vestibulum eius fuit, in 5
quo colossus CXX pedum staret ipsius effigie; tanta
laxitas, ut porticus triplices miliarias haberet. item stagnum maris instar, circumsaeptum est aedificiis ad
urbium speciem; rura insuper arvis atque vinetis et pas-
cuis silvisque varia, cum multitudine omnis generis 10
pecudum ac ferarum. in ceteris partibus cuncta auro
lita, distincta gemmis unionumque conchis erant;
cenationes laqueatae tabulis eburneis versatilibus, ut
flores, fistulatis, ut unguenta desuper spargerentur;
praecipua cenationum rotunda, quae perpetuo diebus 15
ac noctibus vice mundi circumageretur; balineae marinis et albulis fluentes aquis. eius modi domum cum
absolutam dedicaret, hactenus comprobavit, ut se
diceret quasi hominem tandem habitare coepisse.

Suetonius, Nero 31

III The Rebuilding of Rome

The vast destruction of the fire of A.D. 64 enabled Nero to rebuild Rome on a grand scale. Archaeological evidence for this period points to an architectural revolution in building methods, with an emphasis on brick-faced concrete, vaulted buildings, and curvilinear space. This section describes Nero's building program for himself (Part 1); for the rest of the city (Part 2), including the admirable building code that made Rome more resistant to fire and more orderly; and, finally, the people's reaction to Nero's program (Part 3).

To Nero's discredit was his new palace, the Golden House, with which critics both ancient and modern find fault not so much for its opulence, but rather for its extent—a 51-hectare complex of buildings and parkland in central Rome. After Nero's death, the Flavian emperors in a popular move turned most of the complex over to the people with the Colosseum being built on the site of the artificial pond (*stagnum*) and the Baths of Titus (A.D. 79-81) on the palace's Esquiline wing. To replace the Golden House as the imperial residence, Domitian (A.D. 81-96) built a new palace on the Palatine Hill which became the official residence of the emperors for 300 years.

Part 1: *domus aurea*

damnosus, a, um wasteful, extravagant
usque, adv. all the way
transitorius, a, um having a passageway
absumptus, a, um destroyed
restitutus, a, um rebuilt
nomino, are, avi call, name
5 *cultus, us, m* elegance of design
suffecerit haec rettulisse Tr. "it will suffice to have related the following details"
colossus, i, m gigantic statue, colossus
laxitas, atis, f extent
miliarius, a, um mile-long
stagnum, i, n pool, pond
instar + gen. like
circumsaeptum est was surrounded
ad speciem Tr. "to give the appearance"
rura Tr. "rural areas"
insuper besides
arvum, i, n ploughed field
vinetum, i, n vineyard
10 *pascuum, i, n* pasture
pecus, udis, f domestic animal
fera, ae, f wild animal
litus, a, um covered, overlaid
distinctus, a, um decorated, adorned

unionumque conchis Tr. "with mother of pearl"
cenatio, onis, f dining room
laqueatus, a, um adorned with a panelled ceiling
tabula, ae, f panel
eburneus, a, um ivory
versatilis, e revolving, rotating
fistulatus, a, um furnished with pipes
spargo, ere strew, scatter, spray
15 *praecipuus, a, um* chief
rotundus, a, um round
perpetuo, adv. constantly
vice + gen. like
mundus, i, m heavens
circumago, ere revolve
balineae, arum, f baths
marinus, a, um sea
albulis...aquis Tr. "with medicinal spring water"
absolutus, a, um completed, finished
dedico, are dedicate
hactenus to this extent
comprobo, are, avi approve

11

PART 2: *RELIQUA URBIS*

ceterum urbis quae domui supererant non, ut post
Gallica incendia, nulla distinctione nec passim erecta,
sed dimensis vicorum ordinibus et latis viarum spatiis
cohibitaque aedificiorum altitudine ac patefactis areis
additisque porticibus quae frontem insularum pro- 5
tegerent. eas porticus Nero sua pecunia exstructurum
purgatasque areas dominis traditurum pollicitus est.
ruderi accipiendo Ostiensis paludes destinabat utique
naves quae frumentum Tiberi subvectassent onustae
rudere decurrerent; aedificiaque ipsa certa sui parte 10
sine trabibus saxo Gabino Albanove solidarentur,
quod is lapis ignibus impervius est; et subsidia
reprimendis ignibus in propatulo quisque haberet; nec
communione parietum, sed propriis quaeque muris
ambirentur. ea ex utilitate accepta decorem quoque 15
novae urbi attulere. erant tamen qui crederent veterem
illam formam salubritati magis conduxisse, quoniam
angustiae itinerum et altitudo tectorum non perinde
solis vapore perrumperentur: at nunc patulam latitu-
dinem et nulla umbra defensam graviore aestu 20
ardescere.

Tacitus, Annals XV.43

Part 2: *reliqua urbis*

(ea) urbis quae Tr. "those parts of the city that"

supersum, esse + *dat.* be left over, survive

Gallica incendia (*i.e.,* in 390 B.C.)

distinctio, onis, f division, demarcation

passim, adv. at random

erecta (sunt) were built

dimensis vicorum ordinibus Tr. "with rows of streets measured out"

cohibitus, a, um limited

patefactus, a, um open

area, ae, f space: probably courtyards inside *insulae* or houses

5 *porticus, us, f* portico: fires could be fought from the roofs of porticoes

insula ae, f apartment building

exstruo, ere, exstruxi, exstructus build

dominus, i, m owner

purgatasque areas Tr. "building sites cleared of rubbish": Suetonius tells us that Nero allowed only his own men to search for valuables in the ashes

rudus, eris, n rubble

Ostiensis, e of Ostia

palus, paludis, f marsh

destino, are choose, fix upon

subvectassent = subvectavissent had transported

onustus, a, um loaded

10 *decurro, ere* sail down

certa sui parte Tr. "up to a certain height"

trabs, trabis, f wooden beam: this probably means stone vaulted structures, which would be beamless

saxo Gabino Albanove Tr. "by stone quarried at Gabii and Alba": these two ancient cities, located near Rome, were famous for superior-quality fireproof volcanic stone (in Italian, *peperino*)

solido, are make solid, strengthen

impervius, a, um impervious: stone and brick-faced concrete became the major structural materials after the fire

subsidium, ii, n aid, provision (*e.g.,* buckets, pumps, increased water supply stations)

reprimo, ere check, curb, restrain

propatulum, i, n open court

communione parietum Tr. "with common walls"

quaeque (aedificia)

proprius, a, um its own

15 *ambio, ire* enclose

affero, afferre, attuli bring, impart

salubritas, atis, f health

conduco, ere, duxi contribute

angustiae itinerum Tr. "the narrowness of the streets"

tectum, i, n roof

perinde, adv. equally

vapor, oris, m heat

perrumpo, ere penetrate, break through

patulus, a, um open

20 *umbra, ae, f* shade

ardesco, ere be scorched

PART 3: COLOSSEUM

hic ubi sidereus proprius videt astra colossus
  et crescunt media pegmata celsa via,
invidiosa feri radiabant atria regis
  unaque iam tota stabat in urbe domus.
hic ubi conspicui venerabilis Amphitheatri   5
  erigitur moles, stagna Neronis erant.
hic ubi miramur, velocia munera, thermas,
  abstulerat miseris tecta superbus ager.
Claudia diffusas ubi porticus explicat umbras,
  ultima pars aulae deficientis erat.   10
reddita Roma sibi est et sunt te praeside, Caesar,
  deliciae populi, quae fuerant domini.

Martial, *Spectacula* II

IV THE ALLEGED CAUSE OF THE FIRE

sed non ope humana, non largitionibus principis aut
deum placamentis decedebat infamia quin iussum
incendium crederetur. ergo abolendo rumori Nero
subdidit reos et quaesitissimis poenis adfecit quos per
flagitia invisos vulgus Christianos appellabat. auctor 5
nominis eius Christus, Tiberio imperitante, per
procuratorem Pontium Pilatum supplicio adfectus erat;
repressaque in praesens exitiabilis superstitio rursum
erumpebat, non modo per Iudaeam, originem eius
mali, sed etiam per urbem quo cuncta undique atro- 10
cia aut pudenda confluunt celebranturque. igitur pri-

(continued on page 16)

Part 3: Colosseum

METRE: ELEGIAC

Martial wrote the *Liber Spectaculorum* in A.D. 80 to commemorate the opening by Titus of the Flavian amphitheatre, known today as the Colosseum, which, with 80 great arches and standing over 48 metres high, could hold 50 000 spectators.

---

sidereus, a, um starry
astrum, i, n heaven
colossus the 37 m statue of Nero was turned into a statue of the sun by Vespasian
cresco, ere rise
pegma, atis, n scaffold (*i.e.*, scaffolding of new buildings like the Colosseum)
celsus, a, um lofty
invidiosus, a, um hated, detested
radio, are shine, beam
5 *conspicuus, a, um* that stands out, visible
erigo, ere erect, raise
moles, is, f massive structure
velocia Tr. "quickly built"
munus, eris, n gift

thermae, arum, f (*i.e.*, the Baths of Titus)
tectum, i, n home, dwelling
ager, agri, m domain
Claudia...porticus probably the colonnade of the large temple of deified Claudius on the Caelian Hill which, before its completion by Vespasian, formed part of Nero's parklands
diffusus, a, um extended, spread out
explico, are display, throw
10 *aula, ae, f* palace
deficientis Tr. "where it came to an end"
reddo, ere, reddidi, redditus restore
praeses, idis, m ruler, protector
deliciae, arum, f delight

IV   The Alleged Cause of the Fire

This account by Tacitus marks the first known recorded official persecution of Christians by the Roman government and the first mention by a pagan author of the origin of Christianity.

---

largitio, onis, f granting of money
deum = deorum
placamentum, i, n means of soothing (the feelings)
decedo, ere cease, abate
infamia, ae, f sinister belief
quin...crederetur Tr. "so that it did not prevent the belief that the fire had been ordered by Nero"
abolendo rumori Tr. "to suppress the rumour"
subdo, ere, subdidi substitute falsely
reus, i, m culprit, criminal (*i.e.*, a scapegoat)
quaesitus, a, um elaborate
5 *flagitium, ii, n* a disgraceful act: the Roman suspicions about Christians

were encouraged by the Christians' habit of keeping to themselves, by the hostile rumour that they practised magic, incest, and cannibalism, and, finally, by their belief in an imminent second coming of their Messiah, accompanied by a universal cataclysm
supplicio adfectus erat had been put to death
exitiabilis, e deadly, destructive
superstitio, onis, f superstition: any eastern religion, not Greek, would probably be called a "*superstitio*"
10 *cuncta* everything
atrox, atrocis hideous, horrible
pudendus, a, um shameful
celebrantur Tr. "are constantly practised"

15

mum correpti qui fatebantur, deinde indicio eorum
multitudo ingens haud proinde in crimine incendii
quam odio humani generis convicti sunt. et pereunti-
bus addita ludibria, ut ferarum tergis contecti laniatu 15
canum interirent, aut crucibus adfixi aut flammandi,
atque ubi defecisset dies in usum nocturni luminis ure-
rentur.

hortos suos ei spectaculo Nero obtulerat et circense
ludicrum edebat, habitu aurigae permixtus plebi vel 20
curriculo insistens. unde quamquam adversus sontes
et novissima exempla meritos miseratio oriebatur, tamquam non utilitate publica sed in saevitiam unius
absumerentur.

Tacitus, *Annals* XV.44

AGRICOLA

sequens hiems saluberrimis consiliis absumpta. namque ut homines dispersi ac rudes eoque in bella faciles
quieti et otio per voluptates adsuescerent, hortari
privatim, adiuvare publice, ut templa fora domos
exstruerent, laudando promptos, castigando segnes: 5
ita honoris aemulatio pro necessitate erat. iam vero
principum filios liberalibus artibus erudire, et ingenia
Britannorum studiis Gallorum anteferre, ut qui modo
linguam Romanam abnuebant, eloquentiam con-
cupiscerent. inde etiam habitus nostri honor et fre- 10
quens toga; paulatimque discessum ad delenimenta
vitiorum, porticus et balineas et conviviorum elegan-
tiam. idque apud imperitos humanitas vocabatur, cum
pars servitutis esset.

Tacitus, *Agricola* 21

corripio, ere, ripui, reptus bring to trial
fateor, eri confess, admit the charge
indicium, ii, n information
proinde, adv. equally
crimen, inis, n charge
incendium, ii, n burning
odium, i, n hate: a probable explanation
   is the Christians' refraining from public
   spectacles and social gatherings
15 ludibrium, ii, n mockery
tergum, i, n hide
contego, ere, contexi, contectus cover
laniatus, us, m tearing to pieces
intereo, ire die
crux, crucis, f cross
adfixus, a, um fastened to

flammo, are burn, set on fire: burning
   alive was the regular penalty for arson
deficio, ere, defeci die out, wane
lumen, inis, n source of light
uro, ere burn
20 ludicrum, i, n show, spectacle
auriga, ae, f charioteer
permixtus plebi mingling with the people
curriculum, i, n racing chariot
insisto, ere stand in
sons, sontis guilty
exempla Tr. "forms of punishment"
mereor, eri, meritus sum deserve
tamquam on the ground that
utilitas, atis, f benefit
in saevitiam unius Tr. "to satisfy one
   man's cruelty"
absumo, ere kill

Agricola

The city was the natural political and social unit within the Roman empire. This passage taken from Tacitus' *Agricola* describes the use of the city as an agent of imperialism and Romanization. Agricola was Tacitus' father-in-law and governor of Britain from A.D. 78 to A.D. 84.

saluberrimus, a, um most beneficial
consilium, ii, n measure
absumpta = absumpta est
absumo, ere, absumpsi, absumptus pass,
   spend
dispersus, a, um scattered
rudis, e wild, untrained
eo for that reason
faciles = proni
otium, ii, n leisure
voluptas, atis, f pleasure
adsuesco, ere be accustomed to
fora: an inscription has been found
   marking the opening of the new forum
   at Verulamium (now St. Albans) in
   A.D. 79 and bearing Agricola's name
domos: Roman rectangular town and
   country houses which replaced the cir-
   cular Celtic huts
5 segnis, e lazy, sluggish
aemulatio, onis, f rivalry, competition
pro necessitate Tr. "in place of force"
iam vero further

erudio, ire educate
ingenium, ii, n natural ability
studia, orum, n. pl. trained skills
anteferro, anteferre prefer
abnuo, ere reject, treat with disdain
10 concupisco, ere covet: inscriptions reveal
   that Roman jurists arrived in Britain
   after A.D. 80 to set up the law courts
habitus nostri honor (apud eos erat)
paulatim gradually, step by step
discessum = discessum est they went
   astray
delenimentum, i, n allurement
vitium, ii, n vice
balineae, arum, f. pl. baths: excavations
   at Aquae Sulis (Bath) and Silchester
   have been dated to the first century
   A.D.
convivium, ii, n banquet
apud imperitos in the presence of the
   ignorant
humanitas, atis, f civilization
servitus, utis, f slavery

PART I: THE CITY—IDEOLOGY AND PLANNING

Initial Questions

Augustus

1. What is Vitruvius' attitude towards Augustus and his building program? What words and phrases describe his attitude?
2. What role does Vitruvius see for his new book in Augustus' ideology and planning in the light of this passage and the following excerpt from the Preface?

    "...because I noticed that you have built and are now building extensively, and that with respect to the future you will exercise care that future public and private buildings will be handed down as a memorial to posterity just the same as our other proud achievements."

The Parts of Architecture

1. What are the parts of architecture?
2. What structures make up the three-fold division of public buildings in a city?
3. What consideration must be given in architecture to strength, utility, and grace? Why are these three elements so important in planning a city?

The Site of Rome

1. What natural advantages does Camillus claim for rebuilding on the original site of Rome?
2. Select phrases from Camillus' speech that appeal to the sentiment and to the reason of his audience.
3. To what does Livy attribute the city's irregular shape?
4. What comments does Livy make about the planning and rebuilding of Rome?

I The Fire Itself

1. Where did the fire start? What encouraged its spread?
2. Consider how Tacitus uses emphatic word order, diction, and imagery to create a mood of terror, panic, fear, and pity in his graphic account of the fire.
3. Is it an unruly mob or some other group that Tacitus is describing in the last sentence in this passage?

II The Aftermath

1. Why could the extent of the fire's damage be described as disastrous?
2. Outline Nero's relief measures for helping the fire's survivors.
3. Why does Tacitus include rumour in this passage? Does it mean that he is more concerned with the behaviour of important individuals than the mere reporting of the actual events?

Part 1: *domus aurea*

1. Describe the unique features of the *"domus aurea"* in terms of size, luxury, extravagance, imagination, and technical ingenuity.
2. What does Nero mean by his statement, *"ut se diceret quasi hominem tandem habitare coepisse"*? What effect does Nero's comment have after the preceding description of the Golden House by Suetonius?
3. Compare the following description of the Golden House by Tacitus with Suetonius's account:

   > Nero, all the same, made use of the ruins and built a mansion in which the jewels and gold—for they are long since familiar and made common by our luxury— were not as much a cause for wonder as the fields and pools, and on this side woods to provide a wilderness, and, on the other, open spaces and lookouts. The superintendents and architects of these projects were Severus and Celer, who had the ingenuity and the audacity to attempt through art even what nature had denied and to foolishly waste an emperor's resources.

   (a) What details seem to have interested Suetonius and Tacitus? Account for their similarity and difference. Which account do you prefer? Why?
   (b) Does either writer sympathize with or show hostility to Nero's building project? to Nero?

Part 2: *reliqua urbis*

1. Describe the new building regulations. What does the new building code tell the reader about the probable cause of the fire and about the ideology and planning of Nero's *"urbs nova"*?
2. How are landscape and buildings adapted to one another in rebuilding the city?

Part 3: Colosseum

1. How does Martial use emphatic word order, diction, exaggeration, alliteration, and imagery to indicate his attitude towards the Colosseum, the Baths of Titus, and the Golden House?
2. What was Martial's attitude to Nero?

IV The Alleged Cause of the Fire

1. (a) Why did Nero blame the Christians for the fire?
   (b) What was Tacitus' attitude towards the Christians?
2. Do you agree with Tacitus' statement that *"per urbem quo cuncta undique atrocia aut pudenda confluunt celebranturque"*?
3. How did the Roman people react to Nero's actions?

Agricola

1. What qualities of a capable administrator does Agricola show in this passage?
2. Is the tone of this passage rational or irrational? Or is it both? Explain your answer.
3. According to this passage, is the city an important agent of Romanization and pacification? Explain your answer.
4. What are Tacitus' views on Agricola, the natives of Britain, and the ethics of Roman imperialism?

Discussion Questions

1. Is what Vitruvius saw as the proper concern of an architect applicable today?
2. Which of the advantages claimed by Camillus for the site of Rome can be claimed for the sites of Toronto, New York, London, or any other metropolitan city?
3. (a) As Tacitus asks the reader, do you think the fire was accidental or was it deliberately started by the emperor?
   (b) On rereading Tacitus' account of the burning of Rome, what impression do you have of the character of Nero? Does Tacitus admire him? Do you?
   (c) To what extent did Tacitus achieve his claim of writing "without anger and favour"?
   (d) Compare and contrast the planning involved in the rebuilding of Rome in 390 B.C. and in A.D. 64.
   (e) How similar or different is Nero's building code to the one found in your own city or district?
4. Compare and contrast the sense of wonder and amazement of the various writers about the new building projects.
5. What do the various writers in this section tell us about the ideology and planning of a city?
6. What did a Roman city look like? What typical urban structures can be found? Where are open parklands and gardens, businesses, public buildings, mansions, theatres, and sports facilities located? How are civic structures built?
7. To what extent are the political issues raised by Tacitus in the *Agricola* and the *Annals* applicable to modern politics?
8. Examine the material evidence found in Roman Britain to assess the work of Agricola and other provincial governors in promoting Romanization.
9. (a) In what ways does archaeology help us to understand the planning, layout, and character of the ancient city? In answering this question examine such sites as Pompeii, Cosa, Leptis Magna, Ostia, Londinium, and Rome.
   (b) Reread Vitruvius' advice on architecture and on the planning of a city. How far has his advice been implemented in the planning of these cities?
10. Are there features common to all ancient cities? Modern cities? Account for any differences between one ancient city and another or between an ancient and a modern city.
11. Why have some Roman cities survived to the present, while others have not?

Further Readings

Ovid prefers the sophisticated Rome of his day with its new Temple of Apollo and palatial mansions to its primitive state when the Senate house was a mere straw hut and the Palatine Hill was mere pasturage: Ovid, *Ars Amatoria* III.113-129.

Aeneas visits Pallanteum, Evander's little settlement on the future site of Rome: Vergil, *Aeneid* VIII.306-369.

Vitruvius describes the appearance, location, walls, and materials of public buildings: Vitruvius, *De Architectura* I.ii,iv-v;II.

Aeneas mounts a hill and marvels at the buildings of the foreign city of Carthage which possesses architectural features of a Roman city: Vergil, *Aeneid* I.421-429.

PART II

URBAN STRUCTURES— FORUM, BASILICA, TEMPLE, MARKET, AND BATHS

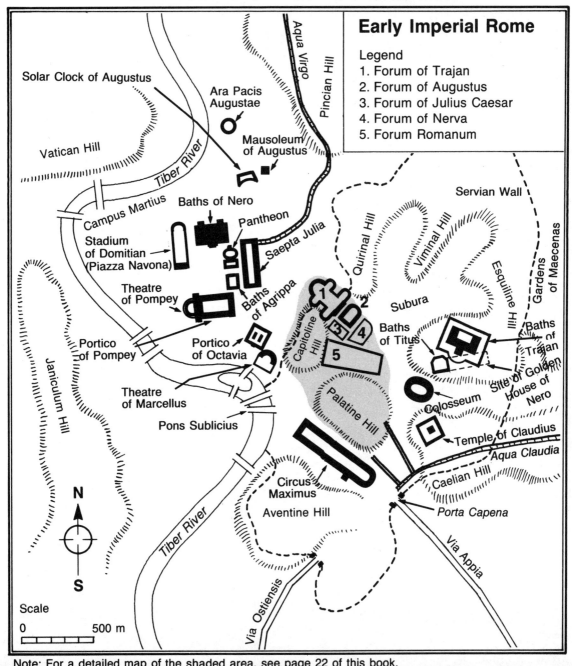

Early Imperial Rome

Legend
1. Forum of Trajan
2. Forum of Augustus
3. Forum of Julius Caesar
4. Forum of Nerva
5. Forum Romanum

Solar Clock of Augustus

Ara Pacis Augustae

Aqua Virgo

Pincian Hill

Vatican Hill

Tiber River

Mausoleum of Augustus

Campus Martius

Baths of Nero

Pantheon

Servian Wall

Quirinal Hill

Viminal Hill

Esquiline Hill

Gardens of Maecenas

Stadium of Domitian (Piazza Navona)

Saepta Julia

Theatre of Pompey

Baths of Agrippa

Subura

Baths of Titus

Baths of Trajan

Portico of Pompey

Portico of Octavia

Capitoline Hill

Site of Golden House of Nero

Janiculum Hill

Theatre of Marcellus

Pons Sublicius

Palatine Hill

Colosseum

Temple of Claudius

Aqua Claudia

Circus Maximus

Caelian Hill

Aventine Hill

Porta Capena

Via Appia

N

S

Scale

0   500 m

Tiber River

Via Ostiensis

Note: For a detailed map of the shaded area, see page 22 of this book.

NOSTALGIA

nec tu credideris urbanae commoda vitae
  quaerere Nasonem, quaerit et illa tamen.
nam modo vos animo dulces reminiscor amici,
  nunc mihi cum cara coniuge nata subit:
aque domo rursus pulchrae loca vertor ad urbis,   5
  cunctaque mens oculis pervidet usa suis.
nunc fora, nunc aedes, nunc marmore tecta theatra,
  nunc subit aequata porticus omnis humo.
gramina nunc Campi pulchros spectantis in hortos,
  stagnaque et euripi Virgineusque liquor.   10

                  Ovid, *Ex Ponto* I.viii.29-38

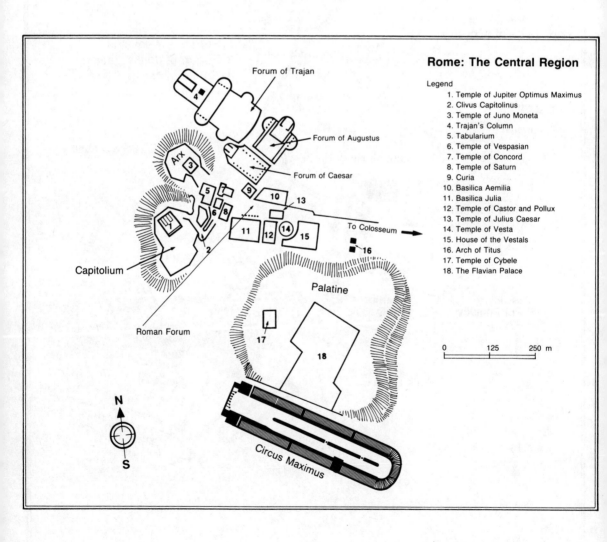

Rome: The Central Region

Legend
1. Temple of Jupiter Optimus Maximus
2. Clivus Capitolinus
3. Temple of Juno Moneta
4. Trajan's Column
5. Tabularium
6. Temple of Vespasian
7. Temple of Concord
8. Temple of Saturn
9. Curia
10. Basilica Aemilia
11. Basilica Julia
12. Temple of Castor and Pollux
13. Temple of Julius Caesar
14. Temple of Vesta
15. House of the Vestals
16. Arch of Titus
17. Temple of Cybele
18. The Flavian Palace

Nostalgia

METRE: ELEGIAC

In exile at Tomis on the Black Sea in A.D. 13, Ovid recalls the majestic grandeur of the gardens, buildings, and colonnades of Rome. Colonnades helped to unify the various public buildings and mansions found in Rome's monumental core of the imperial fora and the Campus Martius. With their fountains, greenery, and statuary, they were a place for pleasant promenades. The Roman taste for landscaping and gardens can be seen in the peristyle of atrium homes, suburban villas, imperial palaces and gardens, and finally the Campus Martius, with its wide-open grass-covered spaces on the banks of the Tiber, affording an escape for the city's inhabitants from the noisy, crowded streets and their hot, dingy apartment quarters. Gardens added to the overall pleasure of city living and were as integral a part of Roman urban architecture as the buildings themselves.

---

nec tu credideris you should not believe

commodum, i, n benefit, advantage

Naso, onis, m Ovid (*i.e.,* Publius Ovidius Naso)

modo...nunc now...now

dulcis, e dear, sweet

reminiscor, reminisci recall to mind, recollect

nata, ae, f daughter

subeo, ire come to mind

5 *aque domo* and from (my) house (*i.e.,* Ovid's house in Rome)

cunctus, a, um every, all

pervideo, ere survey, look upon

fora to accommodate the increase in population and in the number of lawsuits, Augustus added his new Forum Augustus to the existing Forum Romanum and Forum Caesaris (Suetonius, *Augustus* 29)

aedes, is, f temple: Augustus restored 83 temples (Augustus, *Res Gestae* 20)

theatra Augustus repaired the Theatre of Pompey and built the Theatre of Marcellus

aequatus, a, um levelled, made level

porticus, us, f colonnade: a regular feature of forum, temple, and theatre layouts

humus, i, f ground

gramen, inis, n grass

Campus, i, m Campus Martius: used for exercising or walks in the fresh air

10 *stagnum, i, n* pool: probably the Stagnum Agrippae found in the Gardens of Agrippa located in the Campus Martius

specto, are (in + acc) look towards, face

euripus, i, m canal: probably the artificial channel running through the Gardens of Agrippa down to the Tiber

Virgineusque liquor the water of the Aqua Virgo: Agrippa built this aqueduct to supply water for his *Thermae Agrippae*, the first public bath complex in Rome

SALUTATIO

vade salutatum pro me, liber: ire iuberis
   ad Proculi nitidos, officiose, lares.
quaeris iter? dicam. vicinum Castora canae
   transibis Vestae virgineamque domum;
inde sacro veneranda petes Palatia clivo,   5
   plurima qua summi fulget imago ducis.
nec te detineat miri radiata colossi
   quae Rhodium moles vincere gaudet opus.
flecte vias hac qua madidi sunt tecta Lyaei
   et Cybeles picto stat Corybante tholus.   10
protinus a laeva clari tibi fronte Penates
   atriaque excelsae sunt adeunda domus.
hanc pete: ne metuas fastus limenque superbum:
   nulla magis toto ianua poste patet,
nec propior quam Phoebus amet doctaeque sorores. 15
   si dicet "quare non tamen ipse venit?"
sic licet excuses "quia, qualiacumque leguntur
   ista, salutator scribere non potuit."

Martial, Epigrams I.70

salutatio

METRE: ELEGIAC

In order to fulfill his onerous obligation of the early morning *salutatio*, the client, Martial, sends his book from his house on the Quirinal Hill to his patron, Proculus, on the Palatine Hill.

---

vado, ere go

salutatum, a supine Tr. "in order to make a morning call"

nitidus, a, um shiny, gleaming

officiosus, a, um obliging, dutiful

lares, larium, m mansion (lit., household shrine)

iter, itineris, n route

vicinus, a, um + gen. in the neighbourhood of

Castora = templum Castoris

canus, a, um aged

transeo, ire pass by

Vesta the temple of Vesta, the goddess of the hearth, where the Vestal Virgins guarded the sacred fire, which, symbolic of Rome's existence, could never be allowed to go out; the temple's round shape dates back to the huts of primitive Iron Age Rome

virgineam...domum House of the Vestal Virgins: tourists today admire its open colonnaded garden courtyard with roses and three pools filled with goldfish

5 *sacro...clivo* by the sacred slope: part of the Via Sacra ascending from the forum to the Palatine and Capitoline Hills

venerandus, a, um revered, august: because the Palatine Hill (*Palatia*) was the site of the oldest settlement in Rome, and later the residence of the emperors

plurima...imago Tr. "many a statue": in Rome, statues of the reigning emperor, Domitian, could be seen everywhere

detineo, ere delay, detain

radiatus, a, um furnished with rays

colossus, i, m Vespasian had altered a huge bronze statue of Nero (*colossus*) into an image of the Sun-God

Rhodius, a, um the Colossus of Rhodes was one of the seven ancient wonders of the world

moles, is, f massive structure

vinco, ere surpass

flecto, ere bend

hac (parte) (i.e., on the Palatine)

madidus, a, um dripping: a stock epithet of Bacchus (*Lyaeus*), the Wine-God

tectum, i, n roof

10 *Cybeles, Greek gen.* of Cybele, the mother goddess

picto...Corybante Tr. "with its painted Corybants": probably refers to fresco paintings of the priests of Cybele

tholus, i, m dome

protinus, adv. at once

a laeva on the left

clari...fronte with its shiny façade

Penates here, "dwelling" (lit., household gods)

atria the patron, Proculus, would receive clients like Martial in his atrium

excelsus, a, um lofty

metuo, ere fear

fastus, us, m disdain

limen, inis, n threshold

nulla...patet Tr. "no entrance stands with its door leaves wider open": an open door is a symbol of hospitality

15 *nec (ulla domus est)*

propior nearer: here, "more inviting"

doctae sorores the Muses: Roman deities of poetry, music, and dance, and later of all intellectual pursuits

ipse your master

sic licet excuses you may say this in excuse

qualiacumque whatever they are like

salutator, oris, m one who pays a morning call (as a client)

The Capitoline
Temple of Jupiter

I THE KALENDS OF JANUARY

prospera lux oritur: linguis animisque favete!
  nunc dicenda bona sunt bona verba die.
lite vacent aures, insanaque protinus absint
  iurgia; differ opus, livida turba, tuum!
cernis, odoratis ut luceat ignibus aether,   5
  et sonet accensis spica Cilissa focis?
flamma nitore suo templorum verberat aurum
  et tremulum summa spargit in aede iubar.
vestibus intactis Tarpeias itur in arces,
  et populus festo concolor ipse suo est,   10
iamque novi praeeunt fasces, nova purpura fulget,
  et nova conspicuum pondera sentit ebur.
colla rudes operum praebent ferienda iuvenci,
  quos aluit campis herba Falisca suis.
Iuppiter arce sua totum cum spectat in orbem,   15
  nil nisi Romanum, quod tueatur, habet.

Ovid, Fasti I.71-86

I The Kalends of January

METRE: ELEGIAC

On the first of January, the consuls elect entered office. Accompanied by the Senate, they went in solemn procession to the Capitol and there offered sacrifice to Jupiter.

---

prosperus, a, um favourable

lux, lucis, f day

linguis...favete! Tr. "abstain from evil words and evil thoughts" (*i.e.*, keep silent so that no ill-omened word slips out)

lis, litis, f lawsuit: on public holidays, the normal business of the law courts was suspended

vaco, are be free from

vacent...absint: jussive subj.

protinus immediately, forthwith

iurgium, i, n dispute

differo, differe put off

lividus, a, um malicious, rancorous

turba, ae, f crowd (*i.e.*, of suitors)

5 *cerno, ere* see

odoratus, a, um fragrant: because of the incense melted in the sacrificial fire

ut how

luceo, ere glitter, sparkle

aether, eris, m air

sono, are crackle: if the saffron (*spica*) from Cilicia (*Cilissa*) in Asia Minor crackled when thrown into the fire, this was considered a good omen

accensis...focis Tr. "on the blazing hearths"

nitor, oris, m splendour, gleam

tremulus, a, um flickering, quivering

iubar, aris, m radiance

intactus, a, um spotless

Tarpeias...arces Tr. "the Tarpeian towers" (*i.e.*, Ovid uses this part of the Capitoline Hill, from which criminals were thrown, to mean the whole hill with its marble temples)

itur Tr. "the procession goes"

10 *populus...est* Tr. "the people themselves wear the colour of the festive day" (*i.e.*, clothed in white)

praeeo, praeire lead the way

fasces, m rods of office: the consuls were preceded by their lictors carrying bundles of rods and axes (*fasces*), which symbolized their power to inflict flogging or capital punishment

purpura the consuls put on for the first time their purple-bordered togas, the official robe of office

fulgeo, ere shine, gleam

conspicuus, a, um that comes in view, visible

pondus, eris, n weight (of a body)

ebur, oris, n Tr. "ivory chair": consuls, praetors, and curule aediles sat for the first time in the official curule chairs and were carried in solemn procession up the Sacred Way to the Capitol amid the people's cheers

rudis, e inexperienced: young white bullocks (*iuvenci*) being set aside for sacrifice were not made to work or mated

praebeo, ere offer

ferio, ire kill (for sacrifice): annual sacrifice was made to Jupiter for the safety of the Roman state in the upcoming year

aluo, ere, alui graze, feed upon

herba, ae, f grass

Faliscus, a, um of Falerii: an Etruscan country town about 50 km north of Rome, known for its breed of white oxen

16 *tueor, tueri* gaze upon

II THE WORSHIP OF JUPITER

"ego puto omnia a dis fieri. nemo enim caelum caelum putat, nemo ieiunium servat, nemo Iovem pili
facit; sed omnes opertis oculis bona sua computant.
antea stolatae ibant nudis pedibus in clivum, passis
capillis, mentibus puris, et Iovem aquam exorabant. 5
itaque statim urceatim pluebat et omnes redibant udi
tamquam mures. itaque dii pedes lanatos habent, quia
nos religiosi non sumus. agri iacent..."

Petronius, Satyricon 44

BASILICA JULIA

C. PLINIUS ROMANO SUO S.

est mea oratio pro Attia Viriola, et dignitate personae et exempli raritate et iudicii magnitudine insignis.
nam femina splendide nata, nupta praetorio viro,
exheredata ab octogenario patre intra undecim dies, 5
postquam illi novercam amore captus induxerat, quad-
ruplici iudicio bona paterna repetebat. sedebant centum et octoginta iudices tot enim quattuor consiliis
colliguntur: ingens utrimque advocatio et numerosa
subsellia, praeterea densa circumstantium corona latis- 10
simum iudicium multiplici circulo ambibat. ad hoc
stipatum tribunal, atque etiam ex superiore basilicae
parte qua feminae qua viri et audiendi, quod difficile,
et quod facile, visendi studio imminebant. magna
expectatio patrum, magna filiarum, magna etiam 15
novercarum. victa est noverca, ipsa heres ex parte
sexta.

Pliny, Epistulae VI.33

II The Worship of Jupiter

The novelist Petronius, who lived during the reign of Nero, describes in this passage the conversation at Trimalchio's banquet, which has turned to the worship of Jupiter.

---

ieiunium, ii, n fast
Iovis, is, m Jupiter, the god in charge of rain and the weather in general
pili facit Tr. "cares a straw for"
opertus, a, um shut, closed
bona, orum, n. pl. possessions, goods
stolatus, a, um wearing a stola: high-class ladies, clad in *stolae* (ankle-length robes), walked in a religious procession with bare feet and loosened hair (*passis capillis*) as a sign of supplication

clivus, i, m slope: Vitruvius tells us that the temple of Jupiter should be located on a high point, either natural like a hill or artificial like a high podium
5 *urceatim pluebat* Tr. "it began to rain in buckets"
udi tamquam mures Tr. "like drowned rats"
dii pedes lanatos habent Tr. "the gods are slow to aid"
iaceo, ere lie barren

Basilica Julia

Pliny writes to his friend Romanus about a contested will case being heard in the Centumviral Court, which met regularly in the Basilica Julia located on the south side of the Roman Forum.

C. = Gaius
S. = salutem dat sends greetings
dignitas, atis, f position, rank
exemplum, i, n case
raritas, atis, f rarity, unusual nature
iudicium, ii, n court
insignis, e distinguished
nuptus, a, um married
praetorius, a, um of praetorian rank
vir, viri, m husband
5 *exheredo, are, avi, atus* disinherit
octogenarius, a, um eighty-year-old
noverca, ae, f stepmother
induco, ere, induxi bring home
quadriplici iudicio Tr. "united court": the four sets of judges sat together to hear the same case
bona paterna patrimony
repeto, ere sue
iudex, iudicis, m judge
concilia, orum, n. pl. Tr. "chambers"

utrimque on both sides
advocatio, onis, f body of legal assistants
numerosus, a, um crowded
10 *subsellium, ii, n* benches (filled with supporters)
circumstantium Tr. "of onlookers"
corona, ae, f crowd
multiplici circulo Tr. "several rows deep"
ambio, ire surround
ad hoc besides, moreover
stipo, are, avi, atus crowd together
tribunal, is, n the raised platform on which the judges sat at the end of the basilica
ex superiore basilicae parte galleries
qua...qua as well...as
studium, ii, n enthusiasm
15 *immineo, ere* hang down over
heres, heredis, f heiress
ex parte sexta (i.e., for one-sixth of the property of an estate)

A SHOPPING PLACE

in Saeptis Mamurra diu multumque vagatus,
  hic ubi Roma suas aurea vexat opes,
inspexit molles pueros oculisque comedit,
  non hos quos primae prostituere casae,
sed quos arcanae servant tabulata catastae   5
  et quos non populus nec mea turba videt.
inde satur mensas et opertos exuit orbes
  expositumque alte pingue poposcit ebur,
et testudineum mensus quater hexaclinon
  ingemuit citro non satis esse suo.   10
consulit nares an olerent aera Corinthon,
  culpavit statuas et, Polyclite, tuas,
et turbata brevi questus crystallina vitro
  murrina signavit seposuitque decem.
expendit veteres calathos et si qua fuerunt   15
  pocula Mentorea nobilitata manu,
et viridis picto gemmas numeravit in auro,
  quidquid et a nivea grandius aure sonat.
sardonychas veros mensa quaesivit in omni
  et pretium magnis fecit iaspidibus.   20
undecima lassus cum iam discederet hora,
  asse duos calices emit et ipse tulit.

Martial, Epigrams IX.59

A Shopping Place

METRE: ELEGIAC

The *Saepta Iulia*, built of marble and completed in 26 B.C., was a large enclosed area in the Campus Martius that was used as a fashionable shopping place. It was part of Agrippa's newly planned building complex, which included as well the Pantheon, the Basilica of Neptune, and the Baths of Agrippa.

---

vagor, ari, atus sum wander, stroll about

vexo, are make inroads on, ravage

opes, ium, f. pl. wealth, financial resources

mollis, e soft, effeminate: handsome young boys were bought for use as cupbearers and pages

comedo, ere, comedi feast on, devour

primae casae Tr. "outer stalls"

prostituo, ere, ui expose publicly

5 *arcanus, a, um* secret

servo, are reserve

tabulatum, i, n floor

catasta, ae, f a platform on which the slave, often nude, was presented for sale

satur satisfied, satiated

mensa, ae, f a square or rectangular table

opertus, a, um covered

exuo, ere, exui uncover

orbis, is, m round tabletop: Cicero paid 500 000 sesterces for a round table of citrus-wood

expositus, a, um displayed, exhibited

pinguis, e oily, greasy: ivory was polished and rubbed with oil

posco, ere, poposci demand

ebur, oris, n ivory

testudineum...hexaclinon a tortoise-shell dinner-couch for six

mensus, a, um having measured

quater four times

10 *ingemo, ere, ui* sigh

citro...suo Tr. "for his citrus-wood table": an expensive fragrant African wood used in making household furniture

nares, narium, f nose

oleo, ere smell

Corinthon, Greek acc. of Corinthos Corinth

culpo, are, avi blame, condemn

Polyclitus, i, m the great fifth-century B.C. Greek bronze-caster famous for his statues of victorious athletes at Olympia and the Doryphoros (Spear-bearer)

turbata...vitro Tr. "complaining that the crystal was marred by a tiny bit of ordinary glass"

murrina (vasa) murrine vessels: Nero paid 1 000 000 sesterces for a murrine cup; murra was a rare, very expensive opaque stone

signo, are, avi mark (with a seal)

sepono, ere, seposui set aside (i.e., as if Mamurra was intending to buy it)

15 *expendo, ere, di* weigh (i.e, he holds it in his hand and examines it critically)

calathus, i, m a wine cup

Mentoreus, a, um of Mentor: a Greek silversmith of the fourth century B.C.

nobilitatus, a, um made famous

viridis...gemmas Tr. "emeralds"

picto...in auro Tr. "set in embossed gold"

sardonychas, m, Gk. acc. pl. sardonyxes: a precious stone, light to reddish brown in colour, exported from India

20 *pretium facere* to make an offer for

iaspis, idis, f jasper

lassus, a, um exhausted

as, assis, m penny

calix, icis, m cup

ROMA NUPER MAGNA TABERNA FUIT

abstulerat totam temerarius institor urbem
  inque suo nullum limine limen erat.
iussisti tenues, Germanice, crescere vicos,
  et modo quae fuerat semita, facta via est.
nulla catenatis pila est praecincta lagoenis   5
  nec praetor medio cogitur ire luto,
stringitur in densa nec caeca novacula turba
  occupat aut totas nigra popina vias.
tonsor, caupo, coquus, lanius sua limina servant.
  nunc Roma est, nuper magna taberna fuit.   10

Martial, Epigrams VII.61

APER

lintea ferret Apro vatius cum vernula nuper
  et supra togulam lusca sederet anus
atque olei stillam daret enterocelicus unctor,
  udorum tetricus censor et asper erat:
frangendos calices effundendumque Falernum   5
  clamabat, biberet quod modo lotus eques.
a sene sed postquam patruo venere trecenta,
  sobrius a thermis nescit abire domum.
o quantum diatreta valent et quinque comati!
  tunc, cum pauper erat, non sitiebat Aper.   10

Martial, Epigrams XII.70

Roma nuper magna taberna fuit

METRE: ELEGIAC

In A.D. 92, Domitian (*Germanicus*) by edict forbade shopkeepers to let their stalls encroach on street space. Martial wrote this epigram on the occasion of the announcement of this edict.

---

temerarius, a, um thoughtless, inconsiderate
institor, oris, m shopkeeper
limen, inis, n entrance
Germanicus, i, m Domitian took this title
  after his expedition into Germany
tenuis, e narrow, cramped
cresco, ere expand, grow
vicus, i, m street
modo recently, just now
semita, ae, f footpath
5 *catenatus, a, um* chained
pila, ae, f pillar (*i.e.,* of a wine shop)
praecingo, ere, nxi, nctus encircle, surround

lagoena, ae, f flagon
lutum, i, n mud
stringo, ere draw
caecus, a, um blind, rash, aimless
novacula, ae, f razor
niger, nigra, nigrum grimy, dirty, black
popina, ae, f cook-shop, restaurant: often the
  poor had no kitchens of their own and had
  to fetch warm food from one of numerous
  eating-houses
caupo, cauponis, m bar-owner, innkeeper
9 *lanius, ii, m* butcher

Aper

METRE: ELEGIAC

---

linteum, i, n linen cloth (here, "towel")
vatius, a, um bowlegged
vernula, ae, f home-born slave
togula, ae, f paltry toga: a diminutive
luscus, a, um one-eyed
anus, us, f old woman
stilla, ae, f a drop
enterocelicus, a, um ruptured
unctor, oris, m anointer: a bath attendant
  who oiled and massaged the body
udor, oris, m drunkard
tetricus, a, um stern, severe
asper, era, erum harsh
5 *frangendos (esse)* ought to be broken
calix, icis, m wine cup
effundendum (esse) should be poured away
Falernum Falernian wine was a choice

Roman wine
lavo, are, avi, lotus bathe
eques, itis, m knight
patruus, i, m uncle
venere = venerunt
trecenta (milia sestertiorum) 300 000 sesterces
thermae, arum, f. pl. warm baths: large
  heated public baths (*thermae*) were huge
  ornamented buildings that, besides baths
  of varied temperatures, included *palaestrae*,
  concert and lecture halls, libraries, art
  galleries, gardens, promenades, and
  restaurants
diatreta, orum, n. pl. embossed cups
valeo, ere have power, influence
comati Tr. "long-haired slaves"
10 *sitio, ire* be thirsty

HOW TO COOL A HOT BATH

si temperari balneum cupis fervens,
Faustine, quod vix Iulianus intraret,
roga lavetur rhetorem Sabineium.
Neronianas hic refrigerat thermas.

Martial, Epigrams III.25

MENOGENES

effugere in thermis et circa balnea non est
   Menogenen, omni tu licet arte velis.
captabit tepidum dextra laevaque trigonem,
   imputet acceptas ut tibi saepe pilas.
colligit et referet laxum de pulvere follem,   5
   et si iam lotus, iam soleatus erit.
lintea si sumes, nive candidiora loquetur,
   sint licet infantis sordidiora sinu.
exiguos secto comentem dente capillos
   dicet Achilleas disposuisse comas.   10
fumosae feret ipse propin de faece lagonae
   frontis et umorem colligit usque tuae.
omnia laudabit, mirabitur omnia, donec
   perpessus dicas taedia mille "Veni!"

Martial, Epigrams XII.82

How to Cool a Hot Bath

METRE: SCAZON (CHOLIAMBIC)

temperor, ari cool down, regulate
balneum, i, n baths: the baths were a common civic structure in imperial cities; to a Roman, rich or poor, in the capital or in a province, the bath meant that personal hygiene was part of the daily afternoon routine before dinner; besides baths in most private homes of the wealthy, each Roman city had a number of small bathing establishments (*balnea*)

ferveo, ere boil
roga (ut)
lavetur = se lavet bathe or wash oneself
refrigero, are cool off
Neronianas Nero built his public baths on the Campus Martius (*"quid Nerone peius? quid thermis melius Neronianis?"* Martial, *Epigrams* VIII.34, 4-5)

Menogenes

METRE: ELEGIAC

est + inf. it is possible
Menogenen, Greek acc. Menogenes
licet + subj. although
ars, artis, f trick
velis you should wish: here, "you should try"
laeva, ae, f left hand
trigon, onis, m trigon-ball: a hard ball used in the game of trigon, which was played by three players standing in triangular formation and rapidly throwing a ball to each other; the winner was the one who caught the most balls
imputo, are + dat. credit to the account (here, "score to"): Menogenes helps some player by catching balls that the player has missed
acceptus, a, um received (here, "caught")
pila, ae, f ball
ut saepe tibi imputet (suas) acceptas pilas
5 *laxus, a, um* soft
pulvis, eris, m dust
follis, is, m large softball, a bladder- ball (*i.e.*, a ball inflated with air)
lotus, a, um bathed
soleatus, a, um wearing sandals

sumo, ere take
nix, nivis, f snow
candidus, a, um white, bright
sinus, us, m bib (lit., the top part of an infant's outer garment)
exiguus, a, um sparse, scanty
secto...dente Tr. "with a comb"
comentem (te) as subject of *disposuisse*
como, ere arrange
capillus, i, m hair, lock
10 *coma, ae, f* hair, lock
fumosus, a, um smoky: smoke and heat were supposed to hasten the aging of wine
propin, n indeclinable Greek acc. aperitif
faex, faecis, f dregs (*i.e.*, from the bottom of the wine-flask (*lagona*))
frons, frontis, f brow, forehead
umor, oris, m moisture, perspiration
colligo, ere wipe
usque, adv. continuously
donec until
perpessus, a, um after having put up with
taedium, i, n irritation, nuisance
veni! come! (*i.e.*, to dinner)

SENECA'S LODGINGS OVER A PUBLIC BATH

peream si est tam necessarium quam videtur silentium
in studio seposito. ecce undique me varius clamor cir-
cumsonat: supra ipsum balneum habito. propone nunc
tibi omnia genera vocum quae in odium possunt aures
adducere. cum fortiores exercentur et manus plumbo 5
graves iactant, cum aut laborant aut laborantem
imitantur, gemitus audio, quotiens retentum spiritum
remiserunt, sibilos et acerbissimas respirationes. cum
in aliquem inertem et hac plebeia unctione conten-
tum incidi, audio crepitum illisae manus umeris, quae 10
prout plana pervenit aut concava, ita sonum mutat.
si vero pilicrepus supervenit et numerare coepit pilas,
actum est. adice nunc scordalum et furem deprensum
et illum cui vox sua in balineo placet. adice nunc eos
qui in piscinam cum ingenti impulsae aquae sono 15
saliunt. praeter istos quorum, si nihil aliud, rectae
voces sunt, alipilum cogita tenuem et stridulam vocem,
quo sit notabilior, subinde exprimentem nec umquam
tacentem, nisi dum vellit alas et alium pro se clamare
cogit; iam biberari varias exclamationes et botularium 20
et crustularium et omnes popinarum institores mer-
cem sua quadam et insignita modulatione vendentes.

Seneca, Epistulae Morales 56.1-2

Seneca's Lodgings Over a Public Bath

The noises coming from a public bath are the subject of Seneca's letter.

---

peream si colloquial phrase: "I can't for the life of me see"

quam videtur as it is thought to be

in studia seposito for one withdrawn to study

circumsono, are resound on every side

balneum, i, n baths

propono, ere imagine

4 *in odium...adducere* make hateful

exerceo, ere keep busy

iacto, are toss, swing

manus plumbo graves dumbbells, lead weights

gemitus, us, m grunt, groan

quotiens as often as

retentus, a, um pent up

spiritus, us, m breath

remitto, ere, remisi release

sibilus, i, m hissing

acerbus, a, um jarring, harsh

respiratio, onis, f breathing

iners, inertis inactive, idle

plebeius, a, um cheap, ordinary

unctio, onis, f massage, rub down

10 *incido, ere, incidi* happen upon

crepitus, us, m noise, smack

illisus, a, um struck, pummelled

umerus, i, m shoulder

prout according to, whether...or

planus, a, um flat

concavus, a, um cupped, hollow

pilicrepus, i, m ball-player

supervenio, ire come over, come along

pila, ae, f ball

actum est I am done for, I've had it

adicio, ere add

scordalus, i, m brawler, quarrelsome fellow

deprehensus, a, um detected, caught

15 *piscina, ae, f* bathing pool

impulsae aquae Tr. "of splashing water"

salio, ire leap

rectae Tr. "natural"

alipilus, i, m a hair plucker: a slave who plucked the hair from the armpits and nostrils of bathers

tenuis, e weak

stridulus, a, um shrill, squeaky, penetrating

quo sit notabilior in order to advertise his presence

subinde, adv. repeatedly

exprimo, ere force out, give vent

vello, ere pluck

ala, ae, f armpit

pro + abl. instead of

20 *iam...vendentes* assume *cogita*

biberarius, i, m man selling drinks

exclamatio, onis, f loud calling

botularius, ii, m a sausage-maker

crustularius, ii, m a pastry-maker

popina, ae, f cook-shop, low-class restaurant

institor, oris, m pedlar, hawker

merx, cis, f goods, merchandise

insignitus, a, um marked, striking

modulatio, onis, f modulation: here "cry"

PART II: URBAN STRUCTURES—FORUM, BASILICA, TEMPLE, MARKET, AND BATHS

Initial Questions

Nostalgia
1. What feelings for his wife and Rome does Ovid reveal in this selection? Pick out words and images that describe the poet's attitude.
2. What urban structures are described by Ovid in lines 7-10? Could these lines be meant to represent various segments of public life and be intended as an implied tribute to Augustus who had redeveloped so much of the city?
3. How do you think a modern exile would remember his or her own home city? Should one be wary of any exile's account?

salutatio
1. How do the precise topographical references add life and interest to the very Roman custom of the *salutatio*?
2. Trace the route of Martial's book as it makes its journey along the Sacred Way to Proculus' house on the Palatine Hill. Describe the landmarks along the route.
3. How does Martial's choice of words and images reflect a tone of solemnity and religiosity?

I The Kalends of January
1. Would the tone of this passage be described as solemn and dignified? If so, explain by selecting words and images to support your answer.
2. Does Ovid the Roman express his own religious feelings about the grand occasion of the Kalends of January?
3. Examine the structure of the passage. How do words describing colour add to the structure and atmosphere of the passage?

II The Worship of Jupiter
1. According to Petronius, what outward signs of the worship of Jupiter and religion in general are his fellow citizens neglecting? What are the consequences of such neglect?
2. Are there any comments made by Petronius that are relevant and topical today? Explain. Do you agree with Petronius' comments about religion? If so, why?

Basilica Julia
1. How does Pliny's choice of words and images build up the excitement and atmosphere of the Centumviral Court?
2. How does Pliny's description of the architectural details of the Basilica Julia contribute to the tone of his letter?

A Shopping Place
1. How do we know that Mamurra was shopping at an exclusive shopping place? Describe some items for sale.

2. Examine Martial's clever choice of verbs to describe the shopping day of Mamurra. What type of customer was Mamurra?
3. Why does Martial use the names of famous artisans?
4. Relate the last two lines to the rest of the poem.

Roma nuper magna taberna fuit
1. How does Martial use diction, word order, exaggeration, and examples to reflect his disgust at the actions of the shopkeepers and his joy at Domitian's edict?

Aper
1. What poetic devices does Martial use to create a visual word picture of poverty and wealth?
2. How does a change in fortune make Aper a different man at the baths?
3. What phrases describe the poverty of Aper?
4. What custom does Aper resent?
5. How do the last two lines relate to the poem's theme?

How to Cool a Hot Bath
1. Comment on Martial's use of juxtaposition and diction to develop his theme.
2. According to Martial, how do you cool a hot bath?

Menogenes
1. What activities will Menogenes participate in and endure at the baths in order to obtain a dinner invitation?
2. Is the structure of the flatteries used by Menogenes in lines 3 to 12 arranged in some climactic order?
3. Consider how Martial uses contrast, emphatic word order, diction, alliteration, and assonance to create a delightful character.
4. Could Menogenes be described as a bore or a pest? some other name today?

Seneca's Lodgings Over a Public Bath
1. Why does Seneca complain about the baths?
2. What sounds does Seneca hear in his lodgings?
3. Why is a philosopher, like Seneca, able to tolerate the noise?

Discussion Questions

1. What do the passages in this section tell the reader about the various Roman civic forms? Do we learn more about the features of the buildings themselves or about life inside them?
2. Do we have shoppers today like Mamurra?
3. Do we learn about the attitudes of the writers in this section to the various civic structures? If so, how do their attitudes differ?
4. What do coin replicas and archaeological excavations tell us about the various buildings mentioned in this section?
5. The following statistics about imperial Rome are taken from the fourth-century document *Notitia Regionum* XIV:

   > Twenty-eight libraries, 6 obelisks, 8 bridges, 7 hills, 8 parks, 11 *fora*, 10 *basilicae*, 11 *thermae* (large heated public baths; e.g., third-century A.D. Baths of Caracalla which covered about 11 hectares and could accommodate 3000 bathers at one time), 856 smaller private baths, 19 aqueducts, 29 chief roads approaching the city gates, 2 circuses, 2 amphitheatres, 2 market halls, 3 theatres, 4 training schools, 5 *naumachae*, 22 major equestrian statues, 80 gold statues of gods, 36 triumphal arches, 423 shrines, 46 602 *insulae*, 1790 private houses, 290 warehouses, 1352 fountains, 254 corn-mills, 46 brothels, 144 public lavatories, and 10 praetorian cohorts.

   (a) Account for the large number of baths and fountains in Rome. Why do we not have the same number of *thermae* in a modern city?

   (b) Considering the selections you have read on the ancient city, what aspects of it are stressed and what aspects are omitted?

   (c) If you were compiling a list of priorities for a modern city, how would that list differ or be similar to the *Notitia Regionum* XIV?

Further Readings

Horace uses the occasion of the formal dedication of Augustus' Temple of Apollo on the Palatine in 28 B.C. to offer his own prayer for health of body and mind and to spend his old age in poetic pursuits: Horace, *Odes* I.31.

Euclio, the miser, returns empty-handed from shopping for a salted fish at the marketplace because he found everything "too expensive": Plautus, *Aulularia* 370-382.

Vitruvius describes the planning and construction of the temple, forum, basilica, and baths: Vitruvius, *De Architectura* III-V

The wealthy freedman, Trimalchio, takes a bath: Petronius, *Cena Trimalchionis* 26-27.

PART III
LIFE IN THE CITY

Drawing from a marble relief showing an Italian hill town with blocks (*insulae*) resembling two-
and three-storied apartment buildings separated by narrow streets, crowding in the area enclosed
by the town wall — a scene not unlike Juvenal's Rome. Villa Torlonia, Avezzano.

UMBRICIUS, WHY ARE YOU MOVING FROM ROME TO CUMAE?

quamvis digressu veteris confusus amici,
laudo tamen, vacuis quod sedem figere Cumis
destinet atque unum civem donare Sibyllae.
ianua Baiarum est et gratum litus amoeni
secessus. ego vel Prochytam praepono Suburae;   5
nam quid tam miserum, tam solum vidimus, ut non
deterius credas horrere incendia, lapsus
tectorum adsiduos ac mille pericula saevae
urbis et Augusto recitantes mense poetas?
sed dum tota domus raeda componitur una,   10
substitit ad veteres arcus madidamque Capenam.

Juvenal, Satires III.1-11

THE COST OF LIVING

pars magna Italiae est, si verum admittimus, in qua
nemo togam sumit nisi mortuus. ipsa dierum
festorum herboso colitur si quando theatro
maiestas tandemque redit ad pulpita notum
exodium, cum personae pallentis hiatum   5
in gremio matris formidat rusticus infans,
aequales habitus illic similesque videbis
orchestram et populum; clari velamen honoris
sufficiunt tunicae summis aedilibus albae.
hic ultra vires habitus nitor, hic aliquid plus   10
quam satis est interdum aliena sumitur arca.
commune id vitium est: hic vivimus ambitiosa
paupertate omnes. quid te moror? omnia Romae
cum pretio.

Juvenal, Satires III.171-184

Umbricius, Why Are You Moving from Rome to Cumae?

METRE: DACTYLIC HEXAMETER

In this selection and the following four passages, the satirist Juvenal vividly describes the plight of the poor and the perils of city living.

digressus, us, m departure

confusus, a, um upset

sedem figere to make his home

Cumae, arum, f. pl. Cumae, located on the bay of Naples, had few inhabitants

destino, are intend

Sibylla, ae, f the Sibyl of Cumae, the legendary prophetess of Apollo and Diana, gave her oracles in a vast cave

ianua, ae, f gateway

Baiae, arum, f. pl. Baiae, a fashionable bathing resort close to Cumae, near Naples

5 *secessus, us, m* retreat

Prochyta, ae, f Prochyta, a barren volcanic island off Cape Misenum

praepono, ere prefer

Subura, ae, f the Subura, a densely populated area north of the Forum, full of noisy shops and large apartment buildings

deterius worse

incendium, ii, n fire: fire was a constant hazard because of the extreme closeness of buildings to each other and the use of wooden structures, portable stoves, and oil lamps

lapsus tectorum adsiduos Tr. "unending collapse of houses"

10 *domus* Tr. "household belongings"

raeda, ae, f a four-wheeled travelling wagon: Umbricius had to load his personal effects at the city gate since wheeled traffic was not allowed in the city during daylight

componitur Tr. "are loaded"

madidus, a, um dripping (*i.e.*, from the Aqua Marcia whose arches passed over the Porta Capena by which the Via Appia led to Capua)

The Cost of Living

METRE: DACTYLIC HEXAMETER

sumo, ere wear

ipsa Tr. "even"

herbosus, a, um grassy

colo, ere spend, experience

si quando if at any time: word order is "si quando ipsa maiestas dierum festorum colitur"

redit = rediit

pulpitum, i, n stage

5 *exodium, ii, n* farce

persona, ae, f mask

pallens, entis pale-coloured: probably white

hiatus, us, m gaping mouth

gremium, ii, n lap

formido, are shudder at, be frightened of

illic there (here, "in the country")

orchestram = decuriones the seats were reserved for senators in Rome and for lo-

cal officials (*decuriones*) in provincial towns

velamen, inis, n clothing

honor, oris, m office

tunicae in Rome, the toga was the required dress for the theatre, whereas in the country, the white tunica (similar to our T-shirt) was adequate

aedilis, is, m aedile: a town magistrate, in charge of public services and taxes

10 *hic...nitor* Tr. "here (in Rome), the splendour (*nitor*) of the dress..."

ultra vires beyond their means

aliena sumitur arca Tr. "is borrowed from someone else's bank account"

vitium, ii, n fault

ambitiosus, a, um pretentious

quid te moror Tr. "what is more," "in short"

URBAN SLUMS

quis timet aut timuit gelida Praeneste ruinam
aut positis nemorosa inter iuga Volsiniis aut
simplicibus Gabiis aut proni Tiburis arce?
nos urbem colimus tenui tibicine fultam
magna parte sui; nam sic labentibus obstat   5
vilicus et, veteris rimae cum texit hiatum,
securos pendente iubet dormire ruina.
vivendum est illic, ubi nulla incendia, nulli
nocte metus. iam poscit aquam, iam frivola transfert
Ucalegon, tabulata tibi iam tertia fumant: 10
tu nescis; nam si gradibus trepidatur ab imis,
ultimus ardebit quem tegula sola tuetur
a pluvia, molles ubi reddunt ova columbae.

Juvenal, Satires III.190-202

Urban Slums

METRE: DACTYLIC HEXAMETER

Roman builders, who excelled in building public structures and mansions of the wealthy, paid less attention to permanence in lower-class housing such as the *insulae*, where for every 26 apartment buildings there was one private house in Rome. A typical flat in a four- or five-storey apartment building consisted of one or two rooms ill supplied with light, heat, water, and drainage.

gelidus, a, um cool

Praeneste, is, f Praeneste, Tibur (Tivoli), Gabii, and Volusinia are quiet country towns near Rome

nemorosus, a, um woody, tree-clad

iugum, i, n ridge

simplicibus Gabiis Tr. "rustic Gabii"

pronus, a, um sloping, leaning

arx, arcis, f citadel

colo, ere dwell, live in

tenuis, e rickety, weak (i.e., inferior)

tibicen, inis, m prop, support

fulcio, ire, fulsi, fultus shore up

5 *sic* (i.e., *tenui tibicine*)

labentibus (aedificiis) Tr. "collapsing buildings": poorly built "*insulae*" were constructed above the legislated limit of 20 m in an effort to alleviate overcrowding

obsto, are keep from falling

vilicus, i, m landlord's agent

rima, ae, f crack, chink

tego, ere, texi paper over, cover

hiatus, us, m opening

securos...ruina = nos securos dormire iubet pendente ruina

pendente...ruina Tr. "with a collapse hanging over our heads"

vivendum est (mihi)

metus, us, m fear

poscit aquam our idiom is shouting "fire!" whereas the Roman idiom is "water!"

frivola bits and pieces (e.g., worthless furniture)

10 *Ucalegon* Tr. "your neighbour": a reference to Aeneid II.311-312; Ucalegon was a Trojan whose house was burned during the Greek sack of Troy

tabulatum, i, n storey

trepidatur Tr. "the alarm is raised"

tegula, ae, f tile (here, means "tiles or tiling")

tueor, eri guard

pluvia, ae, f rain

reddunt Tr. "lay"

columba, ae, f dove, pigeon: he is so high up that he hears the sound of birds and rain and not of human voices

CITY TRAFFIC

plurimus hic aeger moritur vigilando (sed ipsum
languorem peperit cibus inperfectus et haerens
ardenti stomacho); nam quae meritoria somnum
admittunt? magnis opibus dormitur in urbe.
inde caput morbi. raedarum transitus arto   5
vicorum in flexu et stantis convicia mandrae
eripient somnum Druso vitulisque marinis.
si vocat officium, turba cedente vehetur
dives et ingenti curret super ora Liburna
atque obiter leget aut scribet vel dormiet intus   10
(namque facit somnum clausa lectica fenestra),
ante tamen veniet: nobis properantibus obstat
unda prior, magno populus premit agmine lumbos
qui sequitur; ferit hic cubito, ferit assere duro
alter, at hic tignum capiti incutit, ille metretam.   15
pinguia crura luto, planta mox undique magna
calcor, et in digito clavus mihi militis haeret.

Juvenal, Satires III.232-248

ACCIDENTS DO HAPPEN!

scinduntur tunicae sartae modo, longa coruscat
serraco veniente abies, atque altera pinum
plaustra vehunt; nutant alte populoque minantur.
nam si procubuit qui saxa Ligustica portat
axis et eversum fudit super agmina montem,   5
quid superest de corporibus? quis membra, quis ossa
invenit? obtritum volgi perit omne cadaver
more animae.

Juvenal, Satires III.254-261

City Traffic

METRE: DACTYLIC HEXAMETER

The many apartment buildings in Rome wound around 100 km of alleys and streets, two to five metres in width, most of them unpaved, narrow, dirty, smelly, noisy, and crowded with people.

---

vigilando Tr. "from lack of sleep"

languor, oris, m sickness, illness

pario, ere, peperi cause

inperfectus, a, um undigested

haereo, ere cling, clutch

meritoria, orum, n. pl. rented apartments

admitto, ere allow, permit

magnis opibus dormitur Tr. "there is sleep for the wealthy"

5 *arto vicorum in flexu* Tr. "in the narrow winding streets": the winding streets are caused partly by the city's seven hills

stantis convicia mandrae Tr. "abuse coming from the drivers of the herd brought to a standstill" (*i.e.*, because of a traffic jam)

Druso the emperor Claudius (Tiberius Claudius Drusus) had the habit of sleeping through lawsuits when he presided

vitulisque marinis seals: Seneca described Claudius' voice as a hoarse, inarticulate bark like a seal

officium, ii, n an official duty, business

Liburna, ae, f galley: used metaphorically for a litter (*lectica*)

obiter on the way

10 *fenestra, ae, f* window: the curtains of the litter would be drawn shut

unda, ae, f wave: here, a wave of human beings (*i.e.*, a crowd)

lumbus, i, m loin

ferio, ire strike, hit, knock

cubitus, i, m elbow

asser, eris, n litter-pole

15 *tignum, i, n* beam

incutio, ere strike against

metreta, ae, f jar, cask

pinguia crura luto Tr. "legs (are) coated thick with mud"

planta, ae, f sole of the foot

calco, are tread underfoot

in digito...haeret Tr. "the soldier's hobnailed sandal stamps on my toe"

Accidents Do Happen!

METRE: DACTYLIC HEXAMETER

---

scindo, ere tear, rip

sartus, a, um repaired, mended

corusco, are wave, sway

serracum, i, n heavy goods wagon: builders' wagons were allowed in the daytime in Rome

abies, etis, f fir tree

altera...plaustra, poetic pl. Tr. "a second wagon"

nuto, are swagger, totter

alte, adv. from above

minor, ari threaten

procubuit broke down

saxa Ligustica Ligurian marble: from the Luna (Carrara) quarries

5 *axis, is, m* axle

fundo, ere, fudi pour forth, scatter: roads were bumpy and heavy wagons left deep wheel ruts in the paving stones; people must have been trampled by animals, run over by wagons, or struck by debris from windows and toppled wagons

agmen, agminis, n crowd

membrum, i, n limb

os, ossis, n bone

obtritus, a, um crushed

volgi Tr. "of a commoner"

perit disappears utterly, vanish

cadaver, eris, n corpse

anima, ae, f breath of life

PERILS OF THE NIGHT

respice nunc alia ac diversa pericula noctis:
quod spatium tectis sublimibus unde cerebrum
testa ferit, quotiens rimosa et curta fenestris
vasa cadant, quanto percussum pondere signent
et laedant silicem. possis ignavus haberi   5
et subiti casus inprovidus, ad cenam si
intestatus eas: adeo tot fata, quot illa
nocte patent vigiles te praetereunte fenestrae.
ergo optes votumque feras miserabile tecum,
ut sint contentae patulas defundere pelves.   10
ebrius ac petulans, qui nullum forte cecidit,
dat poenas....
ergo non aliter poterit dormire; quibusdam
somnum rixa facit. sed quamvis improbus annis
atque mero fervens cavet hunc quem coccina laena 15
vitari iubet et comitum longissimus ordo,
multum praeterea flammarum et aenea lampas.
me, quem luna solet deducere vel breve lumen
candelae, cuius dispenso et tempero filum,
contemnit....   20
nec tamen haec tantum metuas; nam qui spoliet te
non deerit, clausis domibus, postquam omnis ubique
fixa catenatae siluit compago tabernae.
interdum et ferro subitus grassator agit rem.

                    Juvenal, *Satires* III.268-288; 302-305

Perils of the Night

METRE: DACTYLIC HEXAMETER

Night-time for the majority of Rome's citizens meant confinement to their dingy rooms in their *insulae*. To venture out at night was fraught with danger for the poor and unescorted. The narrow streets were unlit except for moonlight, and robbers lurked in the darkness.

---

respicio, ere consider, be mindful of: "*respice*" is followed by 3 indirect questions—*quod spatium (sit), quotiens...cadant,* and *quanto...signent*

tectum, i, n roof

sublimis, e lofty, high

cerebrum, i, n head

testa, ae, f potsherd, piece of pottery

ferio, ire strike

rimosus, a, um leaky, cracked

curtus, a, um broken

fenestra, ae, f window: Roman houses normally had no ground-level windows facing the street for fear of burglars

vas, vasis, n pot

cado, ere fall

pondus, eris, n weight

signo, are mark

5 *laedo, ere* damage

silex, icis, m pavement

ignavus, a, um negligent

habeo, ere consider, regard

subitus, a, um sudden, unexpected

inprovidus, a, um ill-prepared

intestatus, a, um without a will made

adeo in fact, for indeed

tot...quot so many...as

tot fata = tot fata (sunt)

pateo, ere stand open

vigil, ilis watchful

optes, jussive subj. you should pray

feras, jussive subj. you should bring

10 *sint (fenestrae)*

patulas...pelves shallow basins

defundo, ere empty, pour down

petulans, antis violent, aggressive

caedo, ere, cecidi kill

aliter otherwise

rixa, ae, f brawl

improbus, a, um reckless

15 *mero fervens* flushed with wine

laena, ae, f cloak: both the lined woollen garment and its scarlet (*coccina*) colour point to a wealthy person

multum...flammarum Tr. "a quantity of torches": Rome had no street lighting

aenea lampas Tr. "bronze lamps"

me as for me: emphatic by position

deduco, ere escort: "*deduco*" is the technical word for the clients' escorting of their patrons as a mark of respect or for protection

candela, ae, f candle: a candle, little valued in comparison with a "*lampas*", was often a rope dipped in tallow or pitch

dispenso et tempero Tr. "I regulate sparingly"

19 *filum, i, n* wick

metuas, jussive subj. you should fear

spolio, are rob, strip

fixus, a, um bound fast, secured

catenatus, a, um chained

sileo, ere, ui fall silent

compago, inis, f Tr. "door-shutters"

interdum in the meantime

grassator, oris, m street robber, mugger

At the Patron's Doorstep

                           nunc sportula primo
limine parva sedet turbae rapienda togatae.
ille tamen faciem prius inspicit et trepidat ne
suppositus venias ac falso nomine poscas:
agnitus accipies. iubet a praecone vocari   5
ipsos Troiugenas, nam vexant limen et ipsi
nobiscum. "da praetori, da deinde tribuno."
sed libertinus prior est. "prior" inquit "ego adsum.
cur timeam dubitemve locum defendere, quamvis
natus ad Euphraten, molles quod in aure fenestrae 10
arguerint, licet ipse negem? sed quinque tabernae
quadringenta parant."...
sed cum summus honor finito computet anno,
sportula quid referat, quantum rationibus addat,
quid facient comites quibus hinc toga, calceus hinc est 15
et panis fumusque domi? densissima centum
quadrantes lectica petit, sequiturque maritum
languida vel praegnas et circumducitur uxor.
hic petit absenti nota iam callidus arte
ostendens vacuam et clausam pro coniuge sellam.   20
"Galla mea est" inquit, "citius dimitte. moraris?
profer, Galla, caput. noli vexare, quiescet."
ipse dies pulchro distinguitur ordine rerum:
sportula, deinde forum, iurisque peritus Apollo....
vestibulis abeunt veteres lassique clientes   25
votaque deponunt, quamquam longissima cenae
spes homini; caulis miseris atque ignis emendus.
optima silvarum interea pelagique vorabit
rex horum vacuisque toris tantum ipse iacebit.

                         Juvenal, *Satires* I.95-106; 117-136

At the Patron's Doorstep

METRE: DACTYLIC HEXAMETER

The *sportula*, a kind of regular handout given by a patron to his clients, was a standard feature of Roman society. Originally, clients dined with their patrons, but this practice was discarded when clients became too numerous. Instead, a daily allocation of food in a small basket (*sportula*) was introduced, but this, in turn, was eventually replaced by a fixed sum of money.

---

sportula, ae, f a dole of food or money

primo limine at the outer threshold

turbae rapienda togatae Tr. "ready to be snatched by the crowd dressed in togas"

ille the patron in person

facies, ei, f face

trepido, are tremble

suppositus, a, um impersonating someone else

5 *agnitus* Tr. "only when recognized"

accipies (sportulam)

praeco, onis, m herald: a clerk who calls out the names on the register

Troieuganas Tr. "the old nobility"

libertinus, i, m freedman: Juvenal himself was a freedman's son

cur timeam Tr. "why should I be afraid?"

10 *Euphraten* the Euphrates River in Mesopotamia in modern-day Iraq can be taken as a general term for the East: Juvenal disliked foreigners

molles...in aure fenestrae Tr. "effeminate holes in their ears (for earrings)": an Asiatic practice

arguerint, potential subj. might prove

licet even though

quadringenta (sestertia) 400 000 sesterces: the property qualification of a knight (*eques*)

paro, are bring in

summus honor Tr. "a consul"

refero, referre bring in

ratio, onis, f income (lit., account)

addat supply *sportula* as the subject

15 *comites = clientes* the poor clients who had to wear the toga and shoes (*calceus*) to receive their dole and to accompany their

patron during the day

hinc from this source (*i.e.*, the *sportula*)

panis, is, m bread

fumus, i, m firewood or charcoal (lit., smoke)

densissima...lectica Tr. "litters in crowds"

centum quadrantes the regular amount of a *sportula*: 25 asses or 6 1/4 sesterces

languidus, a, um sick

praegnas, atis pregnant

circumducitur (*i.e.*, from house to house)

petit absenti (uxor sportulam)

ars, artis, f trick

20 *sella, ae, f* sedan chair

citius faster, more quickly

profer...caput show one's head

quiescet Tr. "she'll be asleep"

pulchro...ordine rerum Tr. "a glorious round of activities": used in ironical manner

peritus, a, um + gen. experienced in

Apollo: in the forum of Augustus was a statue of Apollo who naturally was experienced in law because of all the legal activities going on in his presence

25 *lassus, a, um* wearied, tired, exhausted

vota deponunt put aside hope (*i.e.*, the hope of being invited to dinner after their attendance on their patron all day)

homini, dat. of possession

caulis, is, m cabbage

ignis, is, f fuel (*i.e.*, charcoal)

emendus (est)

pelagus, i, m sea

voro, are devour, swallow up

rex (*i.e.*, the patron)

torus, i, m couch

THE NOISES OF ROME

cur saepe sicci parva rura Nomenti
laremque villae sordidum petam, quaeris?
nec cogitandi, Sparse, nec quiescendi
in urbe locus est pauperi. negant vitam
ludi magistri mane, nocte pistores,   5
aerariorum marculi die toto;
hinc otiosus sordidam quatit mensam
Neroniana nummularius massa,
illinc palucis malleator Hispanae
tritum nitenti fuste verberat saxum;   10
nec turba cessat entheata Bellonae,
nec fasciato naufragus loquax trunco,
a matre doctus nec rogare Iudaeus,
nec sulphuratae lippus institor mercis.
numerare pigri damna quis potest somni?   15
dicet quot aera verberent manus urbis,
cum secta Colcho Luna vapulat rhombo.
tu, Sparse, nescis ista nec potes scire,
Petilianis delicatus in regnis,
cui plana summos despicit domus montis,   20
et rus in urbe est vinitorque Romanus
—nec in Falerno colle maior autumnus—
intraque limen latus essedo cursus,
et in profundo somnus et quies nullis
offensa linguis, nec dies nisi admissus.   25
nos transeuntis risus excitat turbae,
et ad cubile est Roma. taedio fessis
dormire quotiens libuit, imus ad villam.

                              Martial, *Epigrams* XII.57

The Noises of Rome

METRE: SCAZON (CHOLIAMBIC)

Martial contrasts the noisy life of a poor client with the peaceful life of a rich patron in his secluded country villa.

---

siccus, a, um dry, arid

rus, ruris, n fields, lands

Nomentum, i, n Nomentum, a town 23 km northeast of Rome

lar, laris, m household god (here, "home," "abode")

villa, ae, f farm

sordidus, a, um poor, humble (*i.e.*, simple or plain)

quiesco, ere rest

5 *pistor, oris, m* baker

aerarius, ii, m coppersmith

marculus, i, m hammer

otiosus, a, um unoccupied, idle: he often waits for customers at his table

quatio, ere shake

Neronia...massa Tr. "with his heap of Nero's coins": Nero's coins are probably mentioned because he debased the coinage

nummularius, i, m money-changer

palux, ucis, f gold dust

malleator, oris, m a beater

10 *tritus, a, um* worn

nitens, entis glittering (*i.e.*, from the gold particles adhering to the mallet (*fustis*))

fustis, is, m lit., club (here, "mallet")

entheatus, a, um raving, fanatic: an adjective applied to priests of Isis, Serapis, Cybele, and Bellona

fasciatus, a, um bandaged

naufragus, i, m shipwrecked sailor: a begging shipwrecked sailor, real or fraudulent, was a common street sight in ancient times

loquax, acis chattering, babbling, talkative

truncus, i, m body

rogo, are beg

Iudaeus, i, m a Jew: Jews were the most professional group of beggars in Rome

sulphuratae...mercis Tr. "of sulphur wares" (e.g., matches or mended broken glassware)

lippus, a, um half blind, bleary-eyed

institor, oris, m pedlar

15 *piger, gra, grum* lazy

damnum, i, n loss

secta...Luna Tr. "the moon under eclipse": an eclipse was attributed to witches and the striking of brass instruments was used to drive away evil spirits

Colchus, a, um magical, enchanting: because Medea, famed as a sorceress, came from Colchis

vapulo, are be attacked, be struck

rhombus, i, m a magician's wheel used for incantations

Petilianis...regnis (*i.e.*, the villa of a certain Petilius on the Janiculum Hill, now owned by Sparsus)

delicatus, a, um spoiled

regnum, i, n estate, domain

20 *cui plana...despicit domus* Tr. "whose ground floor of the house looks down upon"

vinitor, oris, m vine-dresser (*i.e.*, one who tends or prunes grapevines)

autumnus = vindemia vintage

limen, inis, n boundary

latus, a, um spacious, widespread

essedum, i, n a two-wheeled chariot

in profundo Tr. "in the greatest depth"

25 *dies = lux diei*

ad cubile at my bedside

taedium, ii, n weariness

quotiens whenever

libuit it was pleasing

A Nimble Barber

Eutrapelus tonsor dum circuit ora Luperci
  expingitque genas, altera barba subit.

Martial, Epigrams VII.83

A Rich Man's View of the City

C. PLINIUS MINICIO FUNDANO SUO S.

mirum est quam singulis diebus in urbe ratio aut constet aut constare videatur, pluribus iunctisque non
constet. nam si quem interroges "hodie quid egisti?",
respondeat: "officio togae virilis interfui, sponsalia aut   5
nuptias frequentavi, ille me ad signandum testamentum, ille in advocationem, ille in consilium rogavit."
haec quo die feceris, necessaria, eadem, si cotidie fecisse
te reputes, inania videntur, multo magis cum seces-
seris. tunc enim subit recordatio: "quot dies quam frigi-   10
dis rebus absumpsi!" quod evenit mihi, postquam in
Laurentino meo aut lego aliquid aut scribo aut etiam
corpori vaco, cuius futuris animus sustinetur. nihil
audio quod audisse, nihil dico quod dixisse paeniteat;
nemo apud me quemquam sinistris sermonibus car-   15
pit, neminem ipse reprehendo, nisi tamen me cum parum commode scribo; nulla spe nullo timore sollicitor,
nullis rumoribus inquietor: mecum tantum et cum
libellis loquor. o rectam sinceramque vitam! o dulce
otium honestumque ac paene omni negotio pulchrius!   20
proinde tu quoque strepitum istum inanemque discur-
sum et multum ineptos labores, ut primum fuerit oc-
casio, relinque teque studiis vel otio trade. satius est
enim otiosum esse quam nihil agere. vale.

Pliny, Epistulae I.9

A Nimble Barber

METRE: ELEGIAC

Eutrapelus in Greek his name means
   "nimble"
circueo, ire, circui go around
os, oris, n face

expingo, ere rouge, paint
gena, ae, f cheek
subeo, ire grow, sprout

A Rich Man's View of the City

Pliny contrasts his tedious daily round of city activities with his life of leisure at his country villa at Laurentum, 27 km south of Rome.

C. = Gaius
S. = salutem dat sends greetings
singuli, ae, a each, individual
ratio, onis, f account
consto, are agree, be correct
videor, eri seem
pluribus iunctisque Tr. "several successive
   days taken together"
5 *officio togae virilis* Tr. "at a coming-of-age
   ceremony (for a Roman boy)," who reaches
   the age of 15
intersum, esse, fui be present at, attend
sponsalia, ium, n betrothal ceremony
nuptiae, arum, f wedding
frequento, are, avi attend
ad signandum testamentum Tr. "to witness a
   will": seven witnesses were required to sign
   and seal the will
advocatio, onis, f legal assistance (i.e., a lawyer's activities in court)
in consilium Tr. "to act as an assessor":
   skilled lawyers (jurists) like Pliny were chos-
   en to act as associates (assessors) in a trial
   to a *praetor* inexperienced in law
haec...videntur construe as: "*haec videntur
   necessaria (esse) (eo) die quo feceris (sed), si
   reputes te fecisse cotidie, eadem videntur inania (esse)...*"
reputo, are consider
inanis, e pointless, futile
secedo, ere, secessi retire (to the country)

10 *subeo, ire* come to mind
recordatio, onis, f remembrance, thought
frigidus, a, um dull, trivial
evenio, ire + dat. happen
Laurentinum, i, n Pliny's seaside villa near
   Ostia about 29 km from Rome
corpus, oris, n physical exercise
vaco, are be free for, find time for
fultura, ae, f fitness, support
sustineo, ere maintain, sustain
paeniteat (me) I would regret
15 *sinister, tra, trum* unkind, malicious
carpo, ere blame, carp at
reprehendo, ere find fault with
parum commode, adv. not sufficiently well
sollicito, are harass, disturb
rumor, oris, m gossip
inquieto, are disturb
libellus, i, m book
rectus, a, um proper, appropriate
dulcis, e charming, delightful
20 *otium, i, n* leisure
pulcher, chra, chrum fine, glorious
proinde, adv. accordingly, and so
strepitus, us, m din, noise
discursus, us, m running to and fro
ineptus, a, um silly, absurd
studia, orum, n. pl. studies
trado, ere devote
satius est it is better

A NOISY TEACHER

quid tibi nobiscum est, ludi scelerate magister,
  invisum pueris virginibusque caput?
nondum cristati rupere silentia galli:
  murmure iam saevo verberibusque tonas.
tam grave percussis incudibus aera resultant,   5
  causidicum medio cum faber aptat equo:
mitior in magno clamor furit amphitheatro,
  vincenti parmae cum sua turba favet.
vicini somnum non tota nocte rogamus:
  nam vigilare leve est, pervigilare grave est.   10
discipulos dimitte tuos. vis, garrule, quantum
  accipis ut clames, accipere ut taceas?

Martial, Epigrams IX.68

A Noisy Teacher

METRE: ELEGIAC

Martial's morning nap is disturbed by his neighbourhood school.

quid tibi nobiscum est Tr. "what have you to do with us?" (*i.e.*, "why do you disturb us?")

ludi...magister an elementary-school teacher: classes were often held in the open air on a street corner, in a public arcade or, if the teacher could afford it, hired premises at or near one of the "*fora*"

sceleratus, a, um accursed, wicked

caput, capitis, n person

cristatus, a, um crested

rupere = ruperunt broke

gallus, i, m cock: Roman schools regularly began at dawn

murmur, uris, n continuous roaring

verber, eris, n whip, lash: in Roman schools discipline was universally severe

tono, are thunder

5 *tam grave* Tr. "so loudly"

percussus, a, um beaten

incus, incudis, f anvil

aes, aeris, n bronze: the metal used for equestrian statues

resulto, are resound

causidicus, i, m lawyer

faber, fabri, m smith, metal worker

apto, are fit

mitis, e mild, gentle

in magno...amphitheatro the Flavian amphitheatre (Colosseum)

parma, ae, f the small round shield of the Thracian gladiator

sua turba Tr. "its own supporters"

faveo, ere + dat. applaud

vicinus, i, m neighbour

10 *leve est* it is a small matter

pervigilo, are stay awake all night

garrule Tr. "you chatterbox"

HOW TO SPEND YOUR LEISURE TIME

si tecum mihi, care Martialis,
securis liceat frui diebus,
si disponere tempus otiosum
et verae pariter vacare vitae,
nec nos atria nec domos potentum   5
nec lites tetricas forumque triste
nossemus nec imagines superbas;
sed gestatio, fabulae, libelli,
campus, porticus, umbra, Virgo, thermae,
haec essent loca semper, hi labores.   10
nunc vivit necuter sibi, bonosque
soles effugere atque abire sentit,
qui nobis pereunt et inputantur.
quisquam, vivere cum sciat, moratur?

Martial, Epigrams V.20

How to Spend Your Leisure Time

METRE: PHALAECEAN (HENDECASYLLABIC)

In addressing his epigram to his close friend, the senator Iunius Martialis, Martial philosophically describes some urban architectural features and possible leisure activities the two might enjoy if time permitted.

---

securus, a, um free from care

fruor, frui + abl. enjoy

dispono, ere dispose

pariter in each other's company

vaco, are have leisure or time for, apply oneself to

5 *domos* mansions to which clients, like Martial, must go frequently for their dole

potentum = potentium, gen. pl.

lis, litis, f lawsuit

tetricus, a, um severe, gloomy

tristis, e sad: because the forum was often the scene of funerals, litigation, and business losses

nossemus = novissemus we should know

imago, inis, f ancestral bust (*i.e.,* the halls of great people)

gestatio, onis, f riding

fabula, ae, f conversation

libelli, orum, m. pl. bookshop

campus, i, m field: probably the Campus Martius

porticus, us, f colonnade: these colonnades united and framed forums, and provided shade or protection from weather for pedestrians

umbra, ae, f shade

Virgo, inis, f the Aqua Virgo, an aqueduct built to supply the baths of Agrippa in the Campus Martius, today supplies water to the Trevi fountain

thermae, arum, f warm baths

10 *necuter = neuter, tra, trum* neither

soles = dies

inputo, are enter into the account

quisquam anyone

PART III: LIFE IN THE CITY

Initial Questions

Umbricius, Why Are You Moving from Rome to Cumae?
1. Why does Umbricius prefer the loneliness (*solum*) and wretchedness (*miserum*) of Cumae to Rome?
2. Explain Juvenal's use of antithesis and hyperbole to bring out the mood in Rome.

The Cost of Living
1. How effective is Juvenal's contrast of life in the city with life in the country?
2. What does Juvenal mean by his comment, "*omnia Romae cum pretio*," in lines 13-14?

Urban Slums
1. Why does Juvenal mention small Italian towns in lines 1 to 3?
2. Pick out four phrases in this passage that describe the dangers of city housing. In this passage, what does the landlord tell the tenants to do?
3. How does Juvenal use imagery, alliteration, hyperbole, antithesis, and diction to emphasize the tenements of Rome?

City Traffic
1. How does Juvenal make use of metaphor and hyperbole in describing city traffic?
2. Is Juvenal denouncing the city's traffic problems that make big city life almost unbearable?

Accidents Do Happen!
1. Does Juvenal's use of imagery, diction, and hyperbole arouse sympathy for the plight of the poor? Explain your answer.

Perils of the Night
1. What are the dangers described for the poor citizens at night? Do these dangers still exist in cities today?
2. Explain the pun in the word "*intestatus*" in line 7.
3. What is meant by the words "*somnum rixa facit*" in line 14?
4. How does Juvenal's choice of words and word order build up the tone of the passage?

At the Patron's Doorstep
1. What is meant by the words in the last line, "*vacuisque toris tantum ipse iacebit*"?
2. How does Juvenal's use of irony, antithesis, alliteration, repetition, diction, and imagery help to reveal his attitude towards the social custom of the *sportula*?
3. Does Juvenal convey a mood of indignation, contempt and anger? Yes? No? Explain your answer. Do you feel as the poet does?
4. Why do you think Juvenal uses the stylistic device of dialogue in this passage? How effectively does he use this device?
5. To focus on the scene of the *sportula*, Juvenal presents several types of person as a justification for his attitude. Describe and classify these people.
6. Money is the common element in the interrelationship of the people described in this passage. Is it the misuse of money in the client-patron relationship that angers Juvenal most? Yes? No? Explain your answer.

The Noises of Rome
1. Consider how Martial uses emphatic word order, diction, imagery, and antithesis to make his poem effective.
2. Why does Martial retire to his small, unproductive farm in arid Nomentanum?
3. What does Martial mean by his comment, *"ad cubile est Roma"*?

A Nimble Barber
1. How nimble is Eutrapelus? Explain the pun in his name.
2. What effect does Martial achieve by placing *"Eutrapelus tonsor"* at the beginning of the epigram?

A Rich Man's View of the City
1. What activities take up Pliny's day in Rome?
2. Pliny characterizes these activities as useless. Do you think he means it? Do you consider them useless?
3. What effect on Pliny do activities at his country villa have?
4. What unpleasant features of city life are not found at Laurentum? How does Pliny's use of balance and repetition emphasize these features?
5. What advice does Pliny give to his friend Fundanus?
6. Explain the meaning of the last sentence.
7. Was Pliny really tired of Rome? Is there anything Pliny might miss in the country? If not, account for the tone of Pliny's letter.

A Noisy Teacher
1. Examine Martial's use of emphatic word order, parallelism, diction, alliteration, exaggeration, and imagery. Consider how each contributes to the theme of the poem.
2. How does the epigram's tone change before the end of the poem?
3. Explain the meaning of the last line and a half (*vis...taceas*).

How to Spend Your Leisure Time
1. Describe the images of leisure and business Martial uses in the poem. Show that alliteration, repetition and parallelism reinforce these images.
2. Does the reader learn anything about Martial's attitude towards the client-patron relationship from his description of the client's duties in this poem? Explain your answer.
3. What typical urban structures are described here?
4. Is Martial proud of his city or does he display some other feeling towards it? Explain your answer.
5. What does Martial reveal about life in general in this poem? Relate the last four lines of the poem to the rest of the poem.

Discussion Questions
1. To what extent are the passages in this section satirical?
2. Can Juvenal's Rome at night be compared with Toronto, Montreal, Detroit, New York, London or any other large city in the late twentieth century?
3. Is the keynote of Juvenal's *Satire* III, Martial's *Epigrams* 12.57, and Pliny's *Epistulae* I.9 "escape"? Yes? No? Explain your answer. Is each writer's treatment the same?
4. What living conditions in the ancient city of Rome can still be found in large cities today? Are we better off today? Explain your answer.

5. How does one escape from the routine or stress of daily life? Which ways are effective for you? for others? Do you think these methods would have proved useful to Martial or Pliny? Explain your answer.
6. According to regional registers of the fourth century A.D., there were 1797 private homes of the rich in Rome and 46 602 *insulae* for the poor. Discuss the significance of these statistics in the light of Juvenal's comments.
7. Compare the tone and use of humour by Martial and Juvenal in these selections. Account for the differences, if any.
8. Juvenal, Martial, and Pliny show an acute perception of human nature and a vigorous interest in the life around them. Pick out the most vivid images of city or country life in each author's writings. How far do these images depict life today?
9. Comment on the following passage and relate it to the passages on the *sportula*:
    > From the consulship of Gnaeus and Publius Lentulus onwards, whenever the taxes did not suffice, I made distributions of grain and money from my own granary and patrimony, sometimes to 100 000 persons, sometimes to many more. (Augustus, *Res Gestae* 18)
10. How does each author use a series of contrasts and a capacity to vividly convey a visual scene with words to create and sustain his tone and thoughts?
11. Were Juvenal and Martial trying to reform society? That is, were they moralists? Or were they simply describing the life and society of their times?
12. "People, complete with their vices and virtues, symbolize the city they inhabit." Can one make this statement in the light of today's city and what the authors in this section have described about ancient Rome?
13. How have the excavations at Rome, Pompeii, and Ostia added to our knowledge of daily life in the ancient city? How different were the lives of people who lived in these cities from the lives of those who live in cities today? How were they similar?

Further Readings

Martial presents the reader with an hour-by-hour timetable of his daily activities in the city of Rome: Martial, *Epigrams* IV.8

"While you, Juvenal, are burdened with sleepless nights in Rome, I am happy in my native Spain": Martial, *Epigrams* XII.18

If you wish to be permanently disfigured, visit the barber, Antiochus: Martial, *Epigrams* XI.84

PART IV
SPECTACULA

In this dramatic scene from the Colosseum, a fallen gladiator raises his hand in a plea for mercy. Courtesy The Bettmann Archive, Inc.

THE THEATRE OF POMPEY

M. CICERO S.D. M. MARIO

omnino, si quaeris, ludi apparatissimi, sed non tui
stomachi; coniecturam enim facio de meo. quid enim
delectationis habent sescenti muli in "Clytaemnestra"
aut in "Equo Troiano" creterrarum tria milia aut 5
armatura varia peditatus et equitatus in aliqua pugna?
quae popularem admirationem habuerunt, delectatio-
nem tibi nullam attulissent. reliquae sunt venationes
binae per dies quinque, magnificae, nemo negat; sed
quae potest homini esse polito delectatio, cum aut 10
homo imbecillus a valentissima bestia laniatur aut
praeclara bestia venabulo transverberatur? quae
tamen, si videnda sunt, saepe vidisti; neque nos, qui
haec spectavimus, quicquam novi vidimus. extremus
elephantorum dies fuit. in quo admiratio magna erat 15
turbae, delectatio nulla exstitit; quin etiam misericordia quaedam consecuta est atque opinio eius modi,
esse quandam illi beluae cum genere humano
societatem.

Cicero, *Ad Familiares* VII.1.2-3

The Theatre of Pompey

Cicero writes to his friend Marius in 55 B.C. about the games put on by Pompey on the occasion of the dedication of the Theatre of Pompey, the first theatre in Rome to be built of stone. Before its construction, plays were performed on wooden stages erected for the performance and afterwards pulled down.

M. = *Marcus*

S.D. = *salutem dat* sends greetings

omnino certainly, to be sure

ludi, orum, m. pl. public games: the games or spectacles formed part of the normal day of a Roman citizen and, as emperors and ambitious politicians well knew, could have an effect on public opinion

apparatus, a, um splendid, sumptuous

stomachus, i, m stomach, taste

coniectura, ae, f guess

delectatio, onis, f pleasure, delight

sescenti, ae, a six hundred

mulus, i, m mule

Clytaemnestra, Equus Troianus Latin plays

5 *creterra, ae, f* a bowl (for mixing wine: a possible reference to the spoils of Troy)

armatura, ae, f equipment, armour

varius, a, um multi-coloured

peditatus, us, m infantry

equitatus, us, m cavalry

habuerunt Tr. "caused, produced"

adfero, adferre, attuli bring to

venatio, onis, f combat of wild beasts

bini, ae, a twice daily

10 *politus, a, um* refined, educated

imbecillus, a, um weak, feeble

valens, entis powerful, strong

lanio, are tear to pieces, mangle

venabulum, i, n hunting spear

transverbero, are pierce, transfix

neque...quicquam novi Tr. "and...nothing new"

14 *extremus, a, um* last, final

exsto, are, exstiti be conspicuous, be visible

quin etiam nay even

misericordia, ae, f pity, compassion: according to Pliny, the frantic trumpeting of elephants so moved the spectators that they rose and cursed Pompey (Pliny, *Natural History* VIII.21)

consequor, consequi, consecutus sum follow, ensue

belua, ae, f wild beast

societas, atis, f common bond, affinity

A GLADIATORIAL POSTER

D. Lucreti Satri Valentis, flaminis Neronis Caesaris
Augusti fili perpetui, gladiatorum paria XX et D.
Lucreti Valentis fili gladiatorum paria X pugnabunt
Pompeis VI, V, IV, III, pridie Idus Apriles. venatio
legitima et vela erunt.   5
  scripsit Aemilius Celer singulus ad lunam.

C.I.L. 4.3884

AN EYE SPECIALIST

oplomachus nunc es, fueras ophthalmicus ante.
  fecisti medicus quod facis oplomachus.

Martial, *Epigrams* VIII.74

THE PRIDE OF THE ARENA

Hermes Martia saeculi voluptas,
Hermes omnibus eruditus armis,
Hermes et gladiator et magister,
Hermes turba sui tremorque ludi,
Hermes, quem timet Helius sed unum,   5
Hermes, cui cadit Advolans sed uni,
Hermes vincere nec ferire doctus,
Hermes subpositicius sibi ipse,
Hermes divitiae locariorum,
Hermes cura laborque ludiarum,   10
Hermes belligera superbus hasta,
Hermes aequoreo minax tridente,
Hermes casside languida timendus,
Hermes gloria Martis universi,
Hermes omnia solus et ter unus.   15

Martial, *Epigrams* V.24

A Gladiatorial Poster

D. = *Decimus*: the sponsor's name and title are in the genitive case, depending on paria ("pairs... belonging to...")

flaminis...perpetui: reference to the local cult of the emperor: Claudius Caesar; Nero was the adopted son of the emperor (fili Caesaris Augusti)

flamen, flaminis, m priest

fili, Lucreti = *filii, Lucretii (gen. s.)*

5 *legitimus, a, um* regular (*i.e.*, full scale)

velum, i, n awning

singulus, a, um unassisted, alone

Aemilius Celer the signwriter who probably wrote the inscription by moonlight (*ad lunam*)

An Eye Specialist

METRE: ELEGIAC

---

oplomachus, i, m gladiator

ophthalmicus, i, m eye specialist

The Pride of the Arena

METRE: PHALAECEAN (HENDECASYLLABIC)

In Rome, popular gladiators and charioteers were heroes and matinee idols similar to our present-day pop, cinema, and athletic favourites. Hermes is an example of a Roman hero.

Martius, a, um of Mars

saeculum, i, n age

voluptas, atis, f delight, pleasure

eruditus, a, um skilled: Hermes was adept as a Thracian, a *retiarius* or any other type of gladiator

magister, tri, m trainer

turba...ludi Tr. "the terror and awe of his own school"

5 *unus, a, um* alone

ferio, ire give a death blow

subpositicius sibi ipse Tr. "is his own substitute" (*i.e.*, he needs no-one to replace him in combat)

divitiae, arum, f. pl. riches: here, "source of riches," "source of wealth"

locarius, ii, m seat contractor: because all

Rome wants to see Hermes in the arena, scalpers or speculators in seats make fortunes

10 *ludia, ae, f* a gladiator's wife

belliger, era, erum warrior, warlike

aequoreus, a, um sea

minax, acis threatening

cassis, idis, f helmet (*i.e.*, as an *andabata*, a gladiator who fought on horseback and wore a helmet that covered his eyes)

languidus, a, um drooping: a probable reference to either the armour of the *andabata* or the drooping crest of the Samnite's helmet

15 *omnia solus* Tr. "all things in his single self"

ter unus thrice unique (*i.e.*, as a champion in three types of fighting (lines 11-13))

A GLADIATOR'S ATTITUDE TOWARDS THE GAMES

iam dies aderat, iamque ad spectaculum supplicii nostri
populus convenerat, iam ostentata per harenam
periturorum corpora mortis suae pompam duxerant.
sedebat sanguine nostro favorabilis dominus. cum non
fortunam quisquam nosse, non natales, non patrem 5
poterat, una tamen res faceret apud quosdam me mis-
erabilem, quod videbar inique comparatus. certa enim
harenae destinabar victima, nemo munerario vilius
steterat. fremebant ubique omnia apparatu mortis: hic
ferrum acuebat, ille accendebat ignibus laminas, hinc 10
virgae, inde flagella adferebantur. homines piratas
putares. sonabant clangore ferali tubae, inlatisque Libitinae toris ducebatur funus ante mortem. ubique vulnera, gemitus, cruor; totum in oculis periculum.

Pseudo-Quintiliani, Declamationes Maiores IX.6

A CHRISTIAN'S ATTITUDE TOWARDS THE GAMES

ethnici malum et bonum pro arbitrio et libidine inter-
pretantur. sic ergo evenit, ut qui in plateis litem manu
agentem aut compescit aut detestatur, idem in stadio
gravioribus pugnis suffragium ferat, et qui ad cadaver
hominis communi lege defuncti exhorret, idem in 5
amphitheatro derosa et dissipata et in suo sanguine
squalentia corpora patientissimis oculis desuper incum-
bat; immo qui propter homicidae poenam probandam
ad spectaculum veniat, idem gladiatorem ad
homicidium flagellis et virgis compellat invitum, et qui 10
insigniori cuique homicidae leonem poscit, idem gladi-
atori atroci petat rudem et pilleum praemium conferat.

Tertullian, De Spectaculis 21

A Gladiator's Attitude Towards the Games

This excerpt from a rhetorical exercise describes a fight from a gladiator's point of view. The gladiator had been a rich young man who had been captured by pirates and later sold as a slave to a gladiatorial trainer (*lanista*).

---

supplicium, ii, n punishment
ostento, are, avi, atus show, exhibit
harena, ae, f sand
pompa, ae, f ceremonial procession
favorabilis Tr. "hoping to win favour"
dominus, i, m sponsor, presenter
cum although
5 natales, ium, m birth, origin
miserabilis, e worthy of pity
inique comparatus unfairly matched
munerarius, i, m exhibitor of gladiators
vilius steterat Tr. "had cost at a lower rate"
fremo, ere roar, resound
apparatus, us, m instruments, apparatus
10 acuo, ere sharpen

accendo, ere heat
lamina, ae, f iron plate
virga, ae, f rod, stick (for flogging)
flagellum, i, n whip
adfero, adferre bring forward, produce
putares you would have thought
clangor, oris, m clang, sound
feralis, e deadly
inlatisque Libitinae toris Tr. "and with the
   stretchers for the dead being brought in"
duco, ere conduct
funus, eris, n funeral procession
gemitus, us, m groan
cruor, oris, m blood
in oculis before my eyes

A Christian's Attitude Towards the Games

Tertullian of Carthage, an early Christian writer, explains why Christians should not watch gladiatorial combats.

---

ethnicus, i, m pagan, heathen
arbitrium, ii, n will
libido, inis, f pleasure
evenit ut + subj. it turns out that
platea, ae, f broad street
litem manu agentem Tr. "pursuing a quarrel
   by blows"
compesco, ere restrain, check
suffragium, ii, n support
cadaver, eris, n corpse
5 communi lege by a common law
defunctus = mortuus
exhorreo, ere + ad tremble at
derosus, a, um gnawed or nibbled away

dissipatus, a, um reduced to fragments
squalens, entis filthy, dirty, foul
patiens, entis submissive
incumbo, ere devote oneself to
immo yes indeed
homicida, ae, m. or f. murderer
probo, are express approval
10 homicidium, ii, n murder
flagellum, i, n whip
virga, ae, f rod, switch
invitus, a, um unwilling, reluctant
insignis, e notorious
rudis, is, f rod of discharge
pilleum, i, n cap of freedom

SENECA ATTENDS THE GLADIATORIAL GAMES

nihil vero tam damnosum bonis moribus quam in aliquo spectaculo desidere; tunc enim per voluptatem
facilius vitia subrepunt. quid me existimas dicere?
avarior redeo, ambitiosior, luxuriosior? immo vero
crudelior et inhumanior, quia inter homines fui. casu 5
in meridianum spectaculum incidi, lusus exspectans
et sales et aliquid laxamenti quo hominum oculi ab
humano cruore acquiescant. contra est: quicquid ante
pugnatum est, misericordia fuit; nunc omissis nugis
mera homicidia sunt. nihil habent quo tegantur; ad 10
ictum totis corporibus expositi numquam frustra
manum mittunt. non galea, non scuto repellitur ferrum. quo munimenta? quo artes? omnia ista mortis
morae sunt. mane leonibus et ursis homines, meridie
spectatoribus suis obiciuntur. interfectores interfecturis 15
iubent obici et victorem in aliam detinent caedem. exi-
tus pugnantium mors est; ferro et igne res geritur. haec
fiunt dum vacat harena. "sed latrocinium fecit aliquis,
occidit hominem." quid ergo? quia occidit, ille meruit
ut hoc pateretur: tu quid meruisti, miser, ut hoc 20
spectes? "occide, verbera, ure! quare tam timide incur-
rit in ferrum? quare parum libenter moritur? plagis
agatur in vulnera, mutuos ictus nudis et obviis pec-
toribus excipiant." intermissum est spectaculum:
"interim iugulentur homines, ne nihil agatur." 25

Seneca, *Epistulae Morales* 7.2-5

NERO'S PASSION FOR CHARIOT-RACING

equorum studio vel praecipue ab ineunte aetate
flagravit plurimusque illi sermo, quamquam veteretur,
de circensibus erat; et quondam tractum prasinum
agitatorem inter condiscipulos querens, obiurgante
paedagogo, de Hectore se loqui ementitus est. sed cum 5
inter initia imperii eburneis quadrigis cotidie in abaco

(continued on page 72)

Seneca Attends the Gladiatorial Games

damnosus, a, um destructive, ruinous
mores, um, m character
desideo, ere continue sitting
vitium, ii, n vice
subrepo, ere steal upon, creep into
immo vero nay rather
5 *casus, us, m* chance
meridianum spectaculum Tr. "midday games":
  the morning was mainly devoted to wild
  beast hunts and fights and the afternoon
  to gladiatorial combats; at midday, the
  luncheon interval was often filled with
  fights between condemned convicts
incido, ere, incidi drop into
lusus, us, m amusement
sales, um, m witty talk
laxamentum, i, n relaxation
acquiesco, ere find relief from
contra, adv. the opposite, the contrary
misericordia, ae, f pity
nugae, arum, f nonsense
0 *mera homicidia* Tr. "pure and simple
  murder"
tego, ere protect
ictus, us, m blow
numquam frustra manum mittunt Tr. "they
  never strike in vain"
galea, ae, f helmet

scutum, i, n shield
quo for what purpose
munimentum, i, n defence
15 *obicio, ere* throw to
interfector, oris, m killer, slayer
detineo, ere keep back
caedes, is, f slaughter, massacre
geritur Tr. "the whole event takes place": red
  hot brands, pikes, and whips are used to
  prod the condemned criminals to fight
vaco, are be empty
harena = arena: the combat place in the
  amphitheatre was strewn with sand
  (*harena*)
latrocinium, ii, n highway robbery
quid ergo? but why? why then?
mereo, ere, ui deserve
20 *pateo, ere* be clear, evident
verbero, are whip
uro, ere burn
parum, adv. too little, not enough
libenter, adv. willingly, gladly
plaga, ae, f blow
mutuus, a, um inflicted by each on the other
obvius, a, um exposed
intermitto, ere, misi, missus have an inter-
  mission
25 *iugulo, are* kill by cutting the throat

Nero's Passion for Chariot Racing

studium, ii, n enthusiasm, fondness
vel even, one might go so far as to say
praecipae to a greater degree than others
flagro, are, avi be inflamed with a passion,
  be stirred
tractum Tr. "dragged (by the horses)"
prasinum Tr. "of the green team": after
  spreading the amphitheatre's floor with
  precious green stones, Nero performed as
  a charioteer wearing the green colour

agitator, oris, m charioteer
condiscipulus, i, m classmate
queror, i lament, complain
obiurgo, are scold
5 *paedagogus, i, m* tutor
ementior, i, itus untruthfully explain
eburneis quadrigis Tr. "with model ivory
  chariots"
abacus, i, m gaming board

luderet, ad omnes etiam minimos circenses e secessu
commeabat, primo clam, deinde propalam, ut nemini
dubium esset eo die utique affuturum. neque dis-
simulabat velle se palmarum numerum ampliari; quare 10
spectaculum multiplicatis missibus in serum protrahe-
batur, ne dominis quidem iam factionum dignantibus
nisi ad totius diei cursum greges ducere. mox et ipse
aurigare atque etiam spectari saepius voluit positoque
in hortis inter servitia et sordidam plebem rudimento 15
universorum se oculis in Circo Maximo praebuit,
aliquo liberto mittente mappam unde magistratus
solent.

Suetonius, Nero 22

OVID ATTENDS THE RACES: PART 1

"non ego nobilium sedeo studiosus equorum;
   cui tamen ipsa faves, vincat ut ille, precor.
ut loquerer tecum, veni, tecumque sederem,
   ne tibi non notus, quem facis, esset amor.
tu cursus spectas, ego te: spectemus uterque   5
   quod iuvat atque oculos pascat uterque suos.
o, cuicumque faves, felix agitator equorum!
   ergo illi curae contigit esse tuae?
hoc mihi contingat, sacro de carcere missis
   insistam forti mente vehendus equis,   10
et modo lora dabo, modo verbere terga notabo,
   nunc stringam metas interiore rota.
si mihi currenti fueris conspecta, morabor,
   deque meis manibus lora remissa fluent."

Ovid, Amores III.ii.1-14

secessus, us, m retreat (i.e., in the country)
commeo, are go regularly or frequently
propalam, adv. openly
utique, adv. without fail, certainly
0 dissimulo, are conceal, hide
palma, ae, f prize: the palm-wreath was the
    token of victory for the winning charioteer
amplio, are increase
missus, us, m race
in serum into the late hour (of the day)
dominus, i, m owner
dignor, ari deem worthy

greges Tr. "teams"
aurigo, are drive a chariot
15 inter servitia Tr. "amid a body of slaves"
rudimentum ponere to gain a first experience:
    Nero first appeared as a charioteer in A.D.
    59 in the emperor's private circus in the
    imperial gardens (in hortis) in the Vatican
    valley where one now finds St. Peter's
    Square
praebeo, ere, ui present, represent
mappam...solent Tr. "drop the napkin" (i.e.,
    to indicate the start of the race)

Ovid Attends the Races: Part 1

METRE: ELEGIAC

In the form of a dramatic monologue, Ovid, an unenthusiastic racing fan, describes a chariot race which he attends with a girl whom he wishes to know better. He has eyes only for her, she only for a dashing charioteer.

---

nobilis, e lit., noble (here, "thoroughbred")
studiosus, a, um + gen. keen on, eager
vinco, ere win
precor, ari pray: construe Latin as "precor
    tamen ut ille vincat cui ipsa faves"
loquor, loqui speak
5 cursus, us, m race
spectemus, hortatory subj. let us watch
pasco, ere feed, feast
uterque...uterque one...other
quicumqe, quaecumque, quodcumque whoever
agitator equorum, m charioteer
illi...contigit Tr. "it has happened to him"
    (usually of good luck)
curae esse tuae, predicate dat. to be your care
hoc mihi contingat Tr. "were this to be my
    luck"
carcer, eris, m starting stall: the stalls were
    arranged in a curve to give equal advan-
    tage to all

10 insisto, ere + dat. urge on
lora, orum, n reins
dabo Tr. "I shall give out, I shall let loose"
verber, eris, n whip
tergum, i, n back
noto, are mark
stringo, ere graze
meta, ae, f turning post
interior, ius inner
rota, ae, f wheel
mihi, dat. of agent by me
currenti Tr. "as I fly about the course"
conspectus, a, um caught sight of, noticed
moror, ari delay, falter
de + abl. down from
remissus, a, um slackened
fluent Tr. "will fall"

Ovid Attends the Races: Part 2

"maxima iam vacuo praetor spectacula Circo
  quadriiugos aequo carcere misit equos.
cui studeas, video; vincet, cuicumque favebis:
  quid cupias, ipsi scire videntur equi.
me miserum, metam spatioso circuit orbe!   5
  quid facis? admoto proximus axe subit.
quid facis, infelix? perdis bona vota puellae;
  tende, precor, valida lora sinistra manu.
favimus ignavo. sed enim revocate, Quirites,
  et date iactatis undique signa togis.   10
en revocant; at, ne turbet toga mota capillos,
  in nostros abdas te licet usque sinus.
iamque patent iterum reserato carcere postes,
  evolat admissis discolor agmen equis.
nunc saltem supera spatioque insurge patenti: 15
  sint mea, sint dominae fac rata vota meae.
sunt dominae rata vota meae, mea vota supersunt;
  ille tenet palmam, palma petenda mea est."
risit, et argutis quiddam promisit ocellis:
  "hoc satis hic; alio cetera redde loco!"   20

Ovid, *Amores* III.ii.65-84

Ovid Attends the Races: Part 2

METRE: ELEGIAC

vacuus, a, um empty: because the procession had just left the circuit

praetor, oris, m praetor: as the presiding official of the games, he started the chariot races by dropping a white cloth (*mappa*)

Circus, i, m Circus Maximus

quadriiugus, a, um harnessed in fours: the four-horse chariots did seven laps per race (about 8 km) with each lap recorded by seven huge wooden removable eggs or dolphins erected high above the central platform (*spina*); a day's program normally consisted of twenty-four races with each race taking about fifteen minutes to run

studeo, ere + *dat.* support

5 *me miserum* Tr. "ah, poor me!"

spatiosus, a, um wide

circueo, ire round, go around

orbis, orbis, m turn, curve: a wide turn by a driver meant that the chariot behind could come up and overtake him on the inside

admotus, a, um drawn near

axis, is, m axle

subeo, ire approach, come up gradually

perdo, ere lose

votum, i, n wish

tendo, ere pull tight

precor, ari pray

sinister, tra, trum left: because the turning post was on the left

revoco, are call back: the spectators' large outcry could cause a race to be stopped and restarted

Quirites, um, m. pl. Romans

10 *iacto, are, avi, atus* wave

en! look! see!

turbo, are disturb

abdas te licet Tr. "you may hide"

usque all the way, right into

sinus, us, m bosom, fold of the toga

pateo, ere be open

resero, are, avi, atus open, unlock

postis, is, m gate

evolo, are rush out, fly out

admitto, admittere, admisi, admissus release, allow to enter

discolor, oris of different colours: as with football and hockey teams today, charioteers wore the colours of one of the four competing teams (*factiones*) that hired and trained them; team colours were red, white, blue, and green

15 *saltem, adv.* at least

supera Tr. "get past, overtake"

insurgo, ere gallop, accelerate

(fac) sint mea (vota rata) = *fac sint dominae meae vota rata*

fac + *subj.* see that

ratus, a, um fulfilled

supersum, superesse remain, be left

palma, ae, f prize: the prizes for the victor were a palm and a sum of money

argutus, a, um bright, sparkling, inviting

quiddam, n something

ocellus, i, m eye: a diminutive of *oculus*: used here as a term of endearment

20 *reddo, reddere* render, deliver

A CHARIOTEER'S EPITAPH

dis manibus Epaphroditus, agitator factionis russatae,
vicit CLXXVIII, et apud purpuream vicit VIII. Beia
Feicula fecit coniugi suo bene merenti.

C.I.L. 6.10062

THE BLUE CHARIOTEER

vapulat adsidue veneti quadriga flagello
  nec currit: magnam rem, Catiane, facis.

Martial, Epigrams VI.46

PLINY'S ATTITUDE TOWARDS THE RACES

C. PLINIUS CALVISIO SUO S.

omne hoc tempus inter pugillares ac libellos iucundissima quiete transmisi. "quemadmodum" inquis "in
urbe potuisti?" Circenses erant, quo genere spectaculi
ne levissime quidem teneor. nihil novum nihil varium, 5
nihil quod non semel spectasse sufficiat. quo magis
miror tot milia virorum tam pueriliter identidem
cupere currentes equos, insistentes curribus homines
videre. si tamen aut velocitate equorum aut hominum
arte traherentur, esset ratio non nulla; nunc favent 10
panno pannum amant, et si in ipso cursu medioque
certamine hic color illuc ille huc transferatur, studium
favorque transibit, et repente agitatores illos equos
illos, quos procul noscitant, quorum clamitant nomina
relinquent. tanta gratia tanta auctoritas in una vilis- 15
sima tunica, mitto apud vulgus, quod vilius tunica,
sed apud quosdam graves homines; quos ego cum
recordor, in re inani frigida adsidua, tam insatiabiliter
desidere, capio aliquam voluptatem, quod hac volup-
tate non capior. ac per hos dies libentissime otium 20
meum in litteris colloco, quos alii otiosissimis occupationibus perdunt. vale.

Pliny, Epistulae IX.6

A Charioteer's Epitaph

dis manibus Tr. "to the spirits of the departed"
agitator, oris, m driver
factio russata the red team: the emperor Domitian during his reign (A.D. 81-96)

added two new teams with the colours of purple (*purpurea*) and gold (*aurata*) to the existing teams with colours of red, white, blue, and green
merens, merentis deserving

The Blue Charioteer

METRE: ELEGIAC

vapulo, are be flogged, lashed
adsidue constantly, repeatedly
venetus, i, m blue charioteer
quadriga, ae, f four-horsed chariot

flagellum, i, n whip
nec currit Tr. "and yet drops back"
rem Tr. "feat"

Pliny's Attitude Towards the Races

Pliny describes his feelings about the races to his friend Calvisius Rufus, a town councillor of Comum, Pliny's home town.

C. = Gaius
S. = salutem dat sends greetings
pugillares, ium, m writing tablets
libellus, i, m notebook
transmitto, ere, transmisi pass
quemadmodum how?
Circenses (ludi) the Races: Pliny is probably referring to the Circus Maximus, which 15 held 250 000 people
levissime, adv. very slightly
teneo, ere hold, attract
nihil novum (est)
semel once
spectasse = spectavisse
sufficio, ere be enough
quo magis so all the more
miror, ari be astonished or surprised
pueriliter, adv. childishly
identidem, adv. repeatedly
currentes Tr. "galloping"
insisto, ere + dat. stand in
currus, us, m chariot: an ordinary race was between four chariots at one time
traho, ere attract, draw
ratio, onis, f reason
pannus, i, m racing colour: each team had

its own coloured tunic
cursus, us, m race
studium, ii, n enthusiasm
repente suddenly
agitator, oris, m charioteer
noscito, are recognize, distinguish
clamito, are shout repeatedly, clamour
gratia, ae, f influence, popularity
auctoritas, atis, f value, importance
vilis, e worthless, cheap
mitto apud vulgus, a parenthesis Tr. "never mind the common folk"
recordor, ari recall
inanis, e worthless, empty
frigidus, a, um pointless, boring
adsiduus, a, um constant
insatiabiliter, adv. insatiably, tirelessly
desideo, ere sit idle
20 *voluptas, atis, f* pleasure
otium, ii, n leisure
litterae, arum, f. pl. literature
colloco, are occupy, spend
otiosus, a, um useless, idle
otiosissimis occupationibus: an oxymoron
perdo, ere lose, waste

PART IV: SPECTACULA

Initial Questions

The Theatre of Pompey
1. What is Cicero's attitude to theatrical performances and wild-beast hunts?
2. What effect did the elephants have on the spectators?
3. How does Cicero make use of repetition, parallelism and the rhetorical question to help develop his attitude?

A Gladiatorial Poster
1. What do we learn from the gladiatorial poster about dates, the sponsor, number of gladiators, and other entertainment?

An Eye Specialist
1. What is the point of this witty epigram?

The Pride of the Arena
1. How important is the repetition of the word "*Hermes*" for revealing the theme?
2. Where is there a change of emphasis in the poem? If so, why does it occur?

A Gladiator's Attitude Towards the Games
1. How does the gladiator describe the amphitheatre prior to his own fight?
2. Why does he think that he will not win?

A Christian's Attitude Towards the Games
1. What observations does Tertullian make about the behaviour of pagans?
2. What effect do the games have on the audience and the gladiators?

Seneca Attends the Gladiatorial Games
1. According to Seneca, what effect does a mob have on a person's character?
2. How did the fights viewed by Seneca differ from the gladiatorial fights? Why was Seneca so disgusted by what he saw?
3. How does Seneca's imaginary spectator attempt to defend these fights?
4. Do you think that Seneca's attitude towards the mob and the games would be shared by the plebs?

Nero's Passion for Chariot-Racing
1. What anecdotal details about Nero's life reveal his enthusiasm for chariot-racing?
2. Does Suetonius appear to discredit Nero's character by his choice of words, especially verbs? What is your attitude to Nero?
3. What is the point of Suetonius' use of "*minimos,*" "*primo clam, deinde propalam,*" and in the last sentence, "*aliquo liberto...solent*"?
4. According to Suetonius' account, is there anything sinister about Nero's character? Explain your answer.

Ovid Attends the Races: Part 1
1. Why did Ovid attend the races?
2. What effect may Ovid have wished to achieve by his use of assonance in line 1?
3. Why is the charioteer described as *"felix"* in line 7?
4. What is Ovid imagining in lines 9 to 14?

Ovid Attends the Races: Part 2
1. Why is the charioteer called *"ignavo"* in line 9?
2. What does Ovid mean by *"palma petenda mea est"* in line 18?
3. How helpful is the advice given to the charioteer?
4. How effective is the ending of this poem in line 20?
5. What details about racing and the race course are provided in Parts 1 and 2?
6. Why did Ovid choose not to make the girl, the object of his affection, utter a single line in the poem?
7. Who is the girl?
8. Is this an elaborate fantasy going on in the poet's head or is it an actual event?

A Charioteer's Epitaph
1. How many times did Epaphroditus triumph in the Circus?
2. What teams did he represent as a driver?

The Blue Charioteer
1. Why is Catianus performing a "great feat"?

Pliny's Attitude Towards the Races
1. What has Pliny been doing with his time? Why can he pass his time *"iucundissima quieta"*?
2. What word does Pliny use to describe the mentality of the spectator?
3. Examine the letter carefully to see how Pliny uses a rhetorical question, imagery, and repetition to indicate his attitude towards chariot-racing.
4. Why does a crowd go to the races? According to Pliny, what would be an acceptable reason for attending the races?
5. Why are *"pannus," "graves,"* and *"otium"* suitable words for this letter?
6. How does Pliny's use of contrast unify this letter?
7. What shocks Pliny most about the races?
8. What do you think made chariot races so popular among the Roman people? Has Pliny left something out of his letter to account for the races' popularity?
9. Is Pliny a snob? Yes? No? Explain. Does one form another impression about Pliny's character?

Discussion Questions
1. How much of each form of entertainment can we reconstruct from the details given by each writer?
2. Describe and account for the popularity of the games by rereading the passages in this section and by examining archaeological evidence.
3. Compare the writers' attitudes towards the games, the spectators, and life itself. On what points do the writers agree? disagree?
4. What modern parallels to the audiences, forms of entertainment, and sports facilities of ancient Rome can you suggest? Explain your answer.

5. Choose a passage that provokes a startled reaction on the part of the reader and account for the writer's effect.
6. Is there any important difference between gladiatorial games and professional sports like hockey, football, wrestling, and boxing? Explain your answer.
7. What is your attitude towards violence? Do you think violence on the screen leads to violence on the streets? On what do you base your answer?
8.   Really, I think that the characteristic and peculiar vices of this city, a liking for actors and a passion for gladiators and horses, are all but conceived in the mother's womb. When these occupy and possess the mind, how little room has it left for worthy attainments! Few indeed are to be found who talk of any other subjects in their homes, and whenever we enter a classroom, what else is the conversation of the youths. Even with the teachers, these are the more frequent topics of talk with their scholars. (Tacitus, *Dialogues* 29)

    Do you agree or disagree with this comment by Tacitus? Look through the selections in this section to suppport your view. Are there modern parallels for Tacitus' viewpoint?
9. According to Juvenal, the Roman people's sole interests are "*panem et circenses*" (*Satires* X.81). How accurate is Juvenal's assessment in the light of the selections in this section and in "*At the Patron's Doorstep*" in Part III?

Further Readings

Tacitus describes a riot that occurred at a gladiatorial show presented in Pompeii in A.D. 59 by Regulus, a disreputable ex-senator: Tacitus, *Annals* XIV.17

Claudius and Agrippina preside at an elaborate mock naval battle (*naumachia*): Tacitus, *Annals* XII.56

Julius Caesar sponsors a spectacle to honour his victory in the civil war against Pompey: Suetonius, *Divus Iulius* 39.

Martial states that the racehorse Andraemon has greater fame than his own witty epigrams: Martial, *Epigrams* X.10.

Martial describes a "*venatio*," a combat of wild beasts: Martial, *Spectacula* XIX, XXII.

St. Augustine describes in A.D. 383 the conversion to violence of his Christian friend Alypius: St. Augustine, *Confessions* VI.8.

Juvenal ridicules Eppia, a senator's wife, who elopes to Alexandria with a gladiator: Juvenal, *Satires* VI.102ff.

Vitruvius describes the requirements for planning and building a theatre: Vitruvius, *De Architectura* V.iii-ix.